Costa del Sol, Spain

CH00838739

How to use the **Coursefinder**

The Coast is divided into 6 geographical Areas with a Map for each Course

Use the Index on this page to find the Map for your Course

On the Map, follow the Red Line to find the most direct way to the Clubhouse exiting from the main Coast highway, the A7/E15/N340

The Kilometre marker for the Exit point to your golf course is shown on the Map

KM
121

To measure the distance as you travel to the Clubhouse set your car's Kilometre counter to zero when you turn off the A7/E15/N340

4.4 km

The Text Box on the Map page gives you a short description of the type of journey

Please Note: The maps are symbolic representations and not to scale

We'll get you to the tee on time !

This Coursefinder is brought to you by the Costa del Sol Golf News, the only full-colour English-language golf newspaper on Spain's Costa del Sol, keeping golfers in touch in a lively and informative manner. Now, to celebrate our 10th anniversary in 2005, we have published, with the help of our sponsors, this Coursefinder guide.

One of the issues that has produced much controversy amongst golfers over these past years, is the question of 'finding and getting to the golf-course on time' for which signs on the highway saying 'Campo de Golf' and 'Costa del Golf' may not be enough to help first-time visitors find their way.

Letters and e-mails have inundated my desk complaining about the poor sign-posting on and off the highway and the inadequate directions available to golfers trying to find their golf-course.

Thousands of visiting golfers arrive for the first time on the Costa del Sol every year and need to find their way in their hire-car quickly and easily on time to play their round. Management at courses along the coast might also feel more at ease when a party of twenty-four golfers from Dundee or Dublin arrives relaxed and on time.

We, at Golf News, have published what we believe is the definitive golf-course finder, providing clear detailed maps showing, kilometre by kilometre, the simplest way to every golf course on the Costa del Sol. We expect it to save heartache, and headaches, and help to avoid the kind of frustration endured by those visitors who fail to make it to the tee on time!

Now, even if you are travelling after a rushed breakfast or possibly with a slightly sore head from the night before, the Coursefinder will get you to the tee on time.

If the Coursefinder does just that for you then we will also be happy!

Enjoy your golf in this beautiful part of Europe - if we have 'missed out' any useful information from the Coursefinder that you think is required then please let us know - and if you like our publication please also tell us! Many thanks!

Frank A. Bowles
Editor, Costa Del Sol Golf News

Enjoy Playing

MILLION
DOLLAR
HOLE-IN-ONE®

on the Costa del Sol
and
Around the rest of the World

Driving on the Costa del Sol

Setting out the requirements for driving in Spain, like having a licence and insurance valid for Spain, and being aware of Spanish road rules, such as driving on the right, is not the purpose of this guide. It has been assumed that drivers will have made the necessary enquiries and arrangements about paperwork prior to arrival. The following information, including the list of Useful Words, is to help you understand the instructions and phrases you will come across when driving on the Costa del Sol.

Access by A7 / N340 to the golf-courses

The toll motorway, Autovia, the AP7, provides fast connection along the Coast, but to access the golf-courses it is more practical to use the dual-carriageway numbered A7 / E15 / N340.

The distance-markers on the side of the highway are shown in kilometres, starting from the city of Cadiz in the west - the Costa del Sol starts approximately at Km 100 and finishes just east of the City of Malaga.

Some sections of the highway being modernised no longer show Kilometre markers but otherwise a distance marker is displayed every kilometre.

• **On the maps in this book, the Kilometre marker on the A7 / E15 / N340 is shown as the point at which you should exit the highway to get to your golf-course**

The road system

The roads on which you may find yourself travelling on the Costa del Sol vary between full European toll motorway, motorway, dual carriage-way, national highway and minor country roads. The motorway on the Costa del Sol is the A7, with the toll sections being the AP7. The national A7 / E-15 is slowly replacing the original coastal highway N340, *la carretera nacional*, which connects Cadiz in the west to Malaga in the east. The standard of the connecting roads to travel inland being either main roads or country roads, depend on the destination and its surrounding terrain.

Drivers needing to change direction on *la carretera*, should do so at a *cambio de sentido*, which either has feeder roads going off and on, by underpass or by overpass, or are roundabouts. *Cambios de sentido* are only several kilometres distance from each other, so resist the temptation to save time by turning across the road – which in most places is a physical impossibility because of the concrete centre section. Many sections of the main highway have access by roundabout to the *urbanizaciones*, the housing developments on both sides of the highway. The roundabouts assist the vehicles entering from the right into the fast-moving traffic stream.

Please Note

Spain, in line with the rest of Europe and UK, strictly enforces the rules of safe driving, including the control of speeding.

These rules include:

- Zero-tolerance on drink-driving

- Seat-belts to be worn at all times

- Use of mobile phones prohibited whilst driving

Security on the highways in Spain is managed by the Guardia Civil, Traffic Department (*Trafico*) which enforces these rules with on-the-spot fines (*multa*) amongst other measures

...We'll get you
to the tee
on time !

Useful Words

Listed here are a selection of the Spanish words, with their English equivalents, which you may come across when driving on the Costa del Sol.

Abierto	Open
Acceso	Access
Agencia de Viajes	Travel agent
Aire Acondicionado	Air conditioned
Alquiler de Coches	Car hire
Autopista	Motorway
Autovia	Motorway
Avenida	Avenue
Ayuntamiento	Town hall
Bahia	Bay
Barco	Boat
Bienvenido	Welcome
Bomberos	Fire service
Caballo	Horse
Cadenas	Chains
Calle	Street
Cambio de Divisas	Money exchange
Cambio de Sentido	Turning point
Campo de golf	Golf course
Carga	Load
Carnet de Conducir	Driving licence
Carretera	Road
Casa Club	Club house
Casco	Zone
Casco Urbano	Urban zone
Casco Antiguo	Historic quarter
Centro Ciudad	Town centre
Centro Comercial	Shopping centre
Centro Medico	Medical centre
Cerrado	Closed
Cinturón	Seat-belt
Ciudad	Town
Costa	Coast
Correos	Mail
Curva	Corner
Curva peligrosa	Dangerous corner
Descarga	Unload
Dia	Day
Entrada	Entrance
Escuela	School
Espacio Disponible	Space available
Estación Autobuses	Bus station
Estación de Servicio	Service station
Ferretería	Hardware store
Ferrocarril	Railway
Ferry	Ferry
Frenos	Brakes
Gafas	Spectacles, (eye)
Gasoleo	Diesel
Gasolina	Gas, petrol
Gasolinera	Gas station
Gratuito	No charge
Guardia Civil	Civil Guard
Hostal	Small hotel
Hoyo	Hole (golf)
Información	Information
Lavado	Wash
Levante	East, east wind
Libre	Free, unoccupied
Mar	Sea
Mercado	Market
Multa	Fine
Município	Municipality
Museo	Museum
Neumaticos	Tyres
Noche	Night
Occidental	West
Optica	Optician
Oriental	East
Parking Gratuito	Free parking
Parque Bomberos	Fire station
Permiso de Conducir	Driving licence
Peaje	Toll
Peatonal	Pedestrian
Peligro	Danger
Pinchazo	Puncture
Playa	Beach
Policía Local	Local police

Listed here are a selection of the **Spanish** words, with their English equivalents, which you may come across when driving on the Costa del Sol.

Polideportivo	Sports complex	**Salida de Emergencia**	Emergency exit
Polígono Industrial	Industrial estate	Seguro	Insurance
Poniente	West; west wind	Semáforo	Traffic lights
Prensa	Newspapers	Sin Plomo	Unleaded
Propiedad Privado	Private property	Taller	Workshop
Protección Civil	Citizen protection	Tienda	Shop
Provincia	Province	Transbordador	Car ferry
Pueblo	Village	Urbanización (Urb)	Urban complex
Puerto	Port, marina	Urgencia	Emergency
Red de Carreteras	Road network	Velocidad	Speed
Reduzca velocidad	Reduce speed	Venta	Sale, Inn
Refrescos	Refreshments	Verde	Green
Reparación	Repairs	Via de Servicio	Service road
Roja	Red	Viento	Wind
Salida	Exit; way-out	Vivero	Plant nursery

GOLF COURSES	MAP
Alcaidesa	1
San Roque	2
Sotogrande	3
Valderrama	4
Almenara	5
La Reserva	6
La Cañada	7
La Duquesa	8

Jose Hidalgo

NH Almenara Golf-Hotel & Spa

AREA 1 The Area lies between Gibraltar, and its airport, to the west and the town of Estepona to the east. It includes the courses of Valderrama, Almenara, La Reserva and Sotogrande on the Sotogrande estate, which also has a yacht-marina and polo grounds. San Roque is nearby, and also Alcaidesa, the Links course near Gibraltar. La Duquesa is further east towards Estepona, and has a yacht-marina nearby. Main population centres in the area are Gibraltar, the small towns of San Roque and La Linea, the major port town of Algeciras, the resort of Tarifa, and the growing villages of Guadiaro and Sabinillas/Duquesa. Rural and less developed than further along the coast, the area offers courses which are not yet surrounded by housing, except for the courses on the Sotogrande estate. The marinas at Gibraltar and La Duquesa offer a good selection of bars, cafes and restaurants

...We'll get you to the tee on time !

Cartoon : EWON

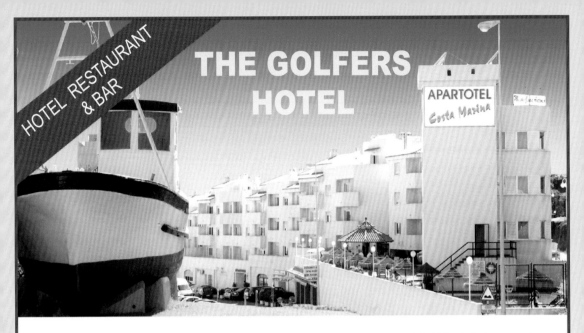

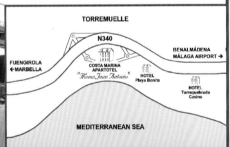

Alcaidesa Links Golf Club

Tel: 956 791 040   Fax: 956 791 041

CN 340 Km 124.6
11315 La Linea, Cadiz

golf@alcaidesa.com
www.alcaidesa.com

METRES	PAR	CV	SLOPE
5766	72	69.6	123
5435	72	68.0	119
4919	72	69.4	113
4579	72	67.5	107

Links course hugging the Mediterranean with spectacular views to Gibraltar and the northern coast of Morocco in Africa. Geographically it is the western most golf course on the Costa del Sol near the towns of San Roque and La Linea.

Features:
Driving Range
Lockers
Storage
Outdoor Patio
Fantastic Views!

Designers:
Peter Alliss
Clive Clark

Opened:
1992

Courtesy Alcaidesa Links Golf Club

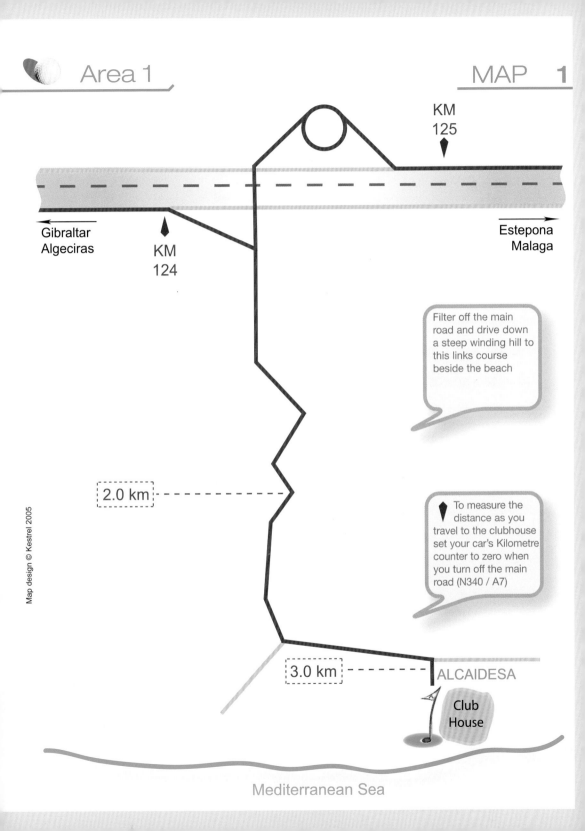

KM
125

Gibraltar
Algeciras

KM
124

Estepona
Malaga

Filter off the main
road and drive down
a steep winding hill to
this links course
beside the beach

Map design © Kestrel 2005

2.0 km

To measure the
distance as you
travel to the clubhouse
set your car's Kilometre
counter to zero when
you turn off the main
road (N340 / A7)

3.0 km ALCAIDESA

Club
House

Mediterranean Sea

San Roque

The San Roque Club

Tel: 956 613 030   Fax: 956 613 305

Urb. San Roque Club, N340 Km.127
11360 Sotogrande, San Roque, Cadiz

info@sanroqueclub.com
www.sanroqueclub.com

Features:
Hotel
Driving Range
Caddies
Pool, Tennis
Squash
Lockers / Storage

Designer:
Dave Thomas

Opened:
Old 1990
New 2004

OLD

METRES	PAR	CV	SLOPE
6497	72	74.1	131
6079	72	72.0	126
5575	72	74.1	125
5010	72	72.3	121

NEW

METRES	PAR	CV	SLOPE
6494	72		
6134	72		
5558	72		
5174	72		

Now a 36-hole complex, San Roque Golf is a high-profile venue with a complete range of facilities to pamper the discerning golfer. It is also normally one of the courses used by the PGA Qualifying School each year.

Courtesy Costa del Sol Golf News

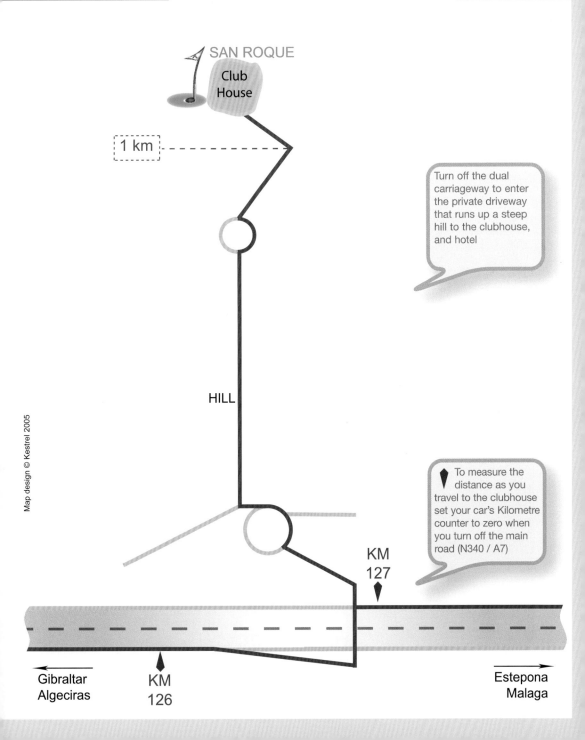

Sotogrande

Royal Sotogrande Golf Club

Tel: 956 785 014 Fax: 956 795 029

Paseo del Parque, N340 Km. 130
11310 Sotogrande, San Roque, Cadiz

reservas@golfsotogrande.com
www.golfsotogrande.com

METRES	PAR	CV	SLOPE
6304	72	73.1	135
5874	72	70.9	131
5425	72	73.9	129
5147	72	72.1	125

Royal Sotogrande was the result of Trent Jones' very first foray into Europe. It is now recognised as being one of the finest golf-courses in Spain and is home to the annual Sherry Cup. Royal Sotogrande, the first, now helps to make up a galaxy of courses open in the area around.

Features:
Driving Range
Caddies
Pool, Tennis
Gym, Sauna
Jacuzzi
Lockers / Storage

Designer:
Robert Trent
Jones Snr

Opened:
1964

Courtesy Costa del Sol Golf News

The course lies on the sea side, south of the main road, just a little way into the south part of the Sotogrande Estate

To
Almenara Golf

La Reserva Golf

Valderrama Golf

To measure the distance as you travel to the clubhouse set your car's Kilometre counter to zero when you turn off the main road (N340 / A7)

A353 Castellar

Guadiaro village

KM 131

Gibraltar Algeciras

KM 130

Estepona Malaga

SOTOGRANDE

Club House

4.0 km

Map design © Kestrel 2005

Valderrama

18

Valderrama Golf Club

Tel: 956 791 200   Fax: 956 796 028

Avda. de Los Cortijos 1
11310 Sotogrande, San Roque, Cadiz

greenfees@valderrama.com
www.valderrama.com

METRES	PAR	CV	SLOPE
6356	71		
5995	72		
5498	72		
4973	72		

Recognised as the No. 1 golf course in Europe, Valderrama hosted the Ryder Cup in 1997, the first time outside the British Isles and Ireland. Valderrama also houses the priceless collection of golfing memorabilia, collected over many years by its owner D. Jaime Ortiz-Patiño.

Features:
Driving Range
Par-3 Course
Caddies

Designer:
Robert Trent
 Jones Snr

Opened:
1985

Almenara Golf

La Reserva Golf

Travel some 3km into the countryside having turned off the main road and crossed via a roundabout and bridge

VALDERRAMA

Club House

To measure the distance as you travel to the clubhouse set your car's Kilometre counter to zero when you turn off the main road (N340 / A7)

2.3 Km

A353 Castellar

Guadiaro village

KM 131

Map design © Kestrel 2005

Gibraltar
Algeciras

KM 130

Estepona
Malaga

NH Almenara Golf-Hotel & Spa
Tel: 956 582 000   Fax: 956 582 001
Avda. Almenara s/n
11310 Sotogrande, San Roque, Cadiz
nhalmenaragolf@nh-hotels.com
www.sotogrande.es

Hotel
Golf Academy
Caddies
Driving Range
Gym, Jacuzzi
Sauna
Nursery, Lockers

Designer:
David Thomas

Opened:
1998

This golf course, close by Valderrama, wends its way through natural parkland surrounded by pine-trees and cork-oaks. The Sotogrande Golf Academy is based here with a driving range and 3-hole course ideal for warm-up purposes. A large natural lake dominates the complex.

ALMENARA A

METRES	PAR	CV	SLOPE
6221	73	73.2	136
5795	73	71.1	134
5177	73	73.4	134
4798	73	71.1	126

ALMENARA B

METRES	PAR	CV	SLOPE
6209	73	73.6	136
5827	73	71.8	131
5263	73	74.8	134
4951	73	72.2	128

ALMENARA C

METRES	PAR	CV	SLOPE
6252	72	73.3	135
5806	72	70.8	135
5336	72	74.4	134
4941	72	71.7	129

Photo: José Hidalgo   Courtesy Costa del Sol Tourist Board www.visitcostadelsol.com

ALMENARA

Club House

Travel some 3 kilometres into the countryside having turned off the main road and crossed via a roundabout and bridge

La Reserva Golf

3.4 km

Valderrama Golf

2.3 km

To measure the distance as you travel to the clubhouse set your car's Kilometre counter to zero when you turn off the main road (N340 / A7)

A353 Castellar

Guadiaro village

KM 131

Map design © Kestrel 2005

Gibraltar Algeciras

KM 130

Estepona Malaga

La Reserva

La Reserva Golf Club

Tel: 956 785 252   Fax: 956 785 272

Avda. de la Reserva s/n
11310 Sotogrande, San Roque, Cadiz

lareserva@sotogrande.es
www.sotogrande.es

METRES	PAR	CV	SLOPE
6448	72	73.6	133
6048	72	71.4	133
5590	72	75.2	132
5104	72	71.9	126

This new course, settling in amongst the elite of Sotogrande, is destined to become one of the great golf-courses in Spain. Opened in the Autumn of 2003, it is located in the heart of the Sotogrande urbanisation. All the greens are designed to USGA standards.

Features:
Hotel
Driving Range
Sauna
Jacuzzi
Lockers / Storage

Designer:
Cabell B.
   Robinson

Opened:
2003

Photo: José Hidalgo

Courtesy Costa del Sol Tourist Board www.visitcostadelsol.com

Almenara Golf

LA RESERVA

Club House

Travel some 3 kilometres into the countryside having turned off the main road and crossed via a roundabout and bridge

3.4 km

To measure the distance as you travel to the clubhouse set your car's Kilometre counter to zero when you turn off the main road (N340 / A7)

Valderrama Golf

2.3 km

A353 Castellar

Guadiaro village

KM 131

Map design © Kestrel 2005

Gibraltar Algeciras

KM 130

Estepona Malaga

La Cañada

La Cañada Golf Club

Tel: 956 794 100   Fax: 956 794 241

Ctra. de Guadiaro Km. 1
11311 Guadiaro-San Roque, Cadiz

cgolflacanada@telefonica.net
www.lacanadagolf.com

METRES	PAR	CV	SLOPE
5841	71	71.5	129
5588	71	70.1	128
4947	71	71.9	125

The only public golf course on the Costa del Sol and produces more Spanish amateur champions than anywhere else in Spain. The first nine holes were designed by Trent Jones and the additional nine by Dave Thomas. The glen on the 9th hole gives its name to the course.

Features:
Driving Range
Caddies
Lockers
Storage

Designers:
Robert Trent
   Jones Snr.
Dave Thomas

Opened:
1982/2001

Courtesy Junta de Andalucia

LA CAÑADA

Club House

2.0 km

Drive less than 2 kilometres off the main road, towards the village and the course is on the way by the side of the road

Avda de los Canos

1.2 km

Calle Altemira

To measure the distance as you travel to the clubhouse set your car's Kilometre counter to zero when you turn off the main road (N340 / A7)

Pueblo Nuevo de Guadiaro village

KM 132

Gibraltar Algeciras

KM 131

Estepona Malaga

La Duquesa

La Duquesa Golf & Country Club
Tel: 952 890 725   Fax: 952 890 725
Urb. El Hacho, N340 Km. 143
29691 Manilva, Malaga
gduquesa@arrakis.es
www.golfladuquesa.com

METRES	PAR	CV	SLOPE
6142	72	71.4	130
5672	72	69.1	132
5207	72	70.6	121
4772	72	69.1	120

Standing on the tee at Hole-8 you have the whole of the Mediterranean before you! This course has wide fairways and large greens to accommodate the average golfer but accurate driving is required. La Duquesa Marina is just opposite.

Features:
Hotel
Driving Range
Tennis, Squash
Pool, Gym
Sauna, Jacuzzi
Lockers, Storage

Designer:
Robert Trent
Jones Snr

Opened:
1986

Courtesy Junta de Andalucia

The course lies just on the north side of the main road

To measure the distance as you travel to the clubhouse set your car's Kilometre counter to zero when you turn off the main road (N340 / A7)

Map design © Kestrel 2005

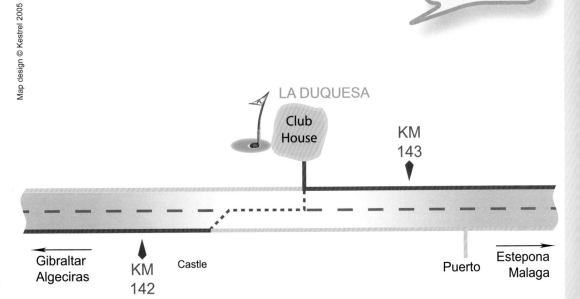

LA DUQUESA

Club House

KM 143

Gibraltar
Algeciras

KM 142

Castle

Puerto

Estepona
Malaga

GOLF COURSES	MAP
Estepona	9
El Coto La Serena	10
Los Flamingos	11
Los Almendros	12
El Paraiso	13
El Campanario	14
Atalaya Park	15
Marbella Club GR	16
Monte Mayor	17
Guadalmina	18

Monte Mayor Golf & Country Club

AREA 2 The Area lies between the town of Estepona to the west and to the east San Pedro, a few kilometres from Marbella. It includes Estepona Golf, near the town of Estepona, and after Estepona the courses at Los Flamingos, El Paraiso and Atalaya Park. A few kilometres inland are the courses of Marbella Club Golf Resort and Monte Mayor and just before San Pedro is Guadalmina. Main population centres in the area are the towns of Estepona and San Pedro de Alcantara, together with, a little way inland, the village of Benahavis, famous internationally for its many gourmet restaurants. Much of the area getting close to San Pedro is built-up but from Estepona it remains mostly rural. The marina at Estepona, and the town centre, offer a good selection of fish restaurants

...We'll get you
to the tee
on time !

UNBELIEVABLE 500 EUROS+ FOR THE WEEK!

DETACHED VILLA   3-4 BEDROOMS
GAMES-ENTERTAINMENT ROOM
PRIVATE GARDEN
PRIVATE POOL
FREE GOLF *
FREE CAR HIRE **
TEE TIME BOOKING SERVICE
MASSAGE / SPORTS INJURY ***
SINGLE/ GROUP GOLF TUITION ***

+ 500 euros covers the community fees for one year
* Free golf for one person during their stay at a course chosen by Tops. Discounted fees available at other courses.
** Free car hire - 307 or equivalent. Upgrades available.
*** Hourly rates apply

Tops Property are proud to offer shares in their Shared Ownership Scheme (SOS) which can be sold on at anytime realising a
profit from as little as 15,000 Euros and in return our clients will benefit from this amazing package.

For more details contact Ann Keeble on 607 864 082 or 952 790 728 or email ann@topsproperty.com

Estepona

Estepona Golf

Tel: 952 937 605   Fax: 952 937 600

Apdo 532, Arroyo Vaquero, N340 Km.150
29680 Estepona, Malaga

information@esteponagolf.com
www.esteponagolf.com

METRES	PAR	CV	SLOPE
6001	72	71.3	134
5610	72	69.6	130
5137	72	70.9	123

Known as the 'friendliest course on the coast' Estepona Golf is a well-run family business and good value for money. The 3rd hole – the ski-run – is the longest in Spain measuring 568m from the white tees. The course nestles in the foothills of the Sierra Bermeja.

Features:
Hotel
Driving Range
Gym
Jacuzzi
Lockers

Designer:
Jose-Luis
    Lopez Martinez

Opened:
1989

Photo: José Hidalgo

Courtesy Costa del Sol Tourist Board www.visitcostadelsol.com

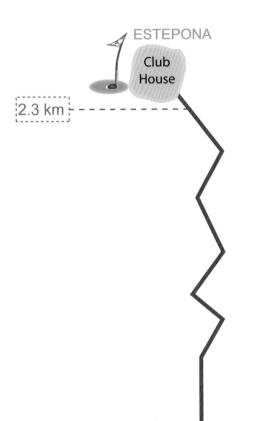

ESTEPONA

Club House

2.3 km

The exit from the main road is an abrupt one and the turn off, immediately after the 150 KM marker, should be approached with care

To measure the distance as you travel to the clubhouse set your car's Kilometre counter to zero when you turn off the main road (N340 / A7)

KM 150

Gibraltar
Algeciras

 KM 149

Estepona
Malaga

El Coto de La Serena Golf Club

Tel: 952 874 700   Fax: 952 804 708

Ctra. de Cadiz (N340) Km 163.5
29680 Estepona, Malaga

coto@golf-andalucia.net

Features:
Driving Range
Lockers
Dressing Room
Club Rental

Designer:
Pedro Moran

Opened:
1989

The streams crossing the fairways give the course a peaceful atmosphere - and call for accuracy on the Par 3's.

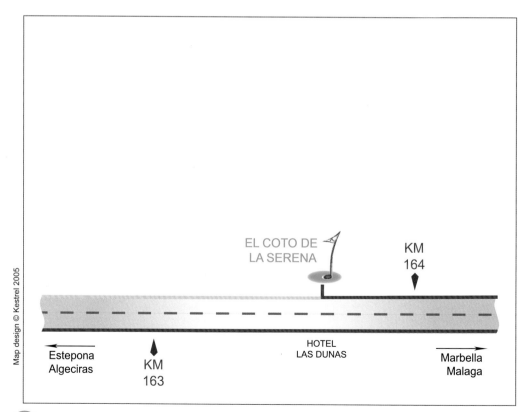

EL COTO DE
LA SERENA

KM
164

HOTEL
LAS DUNAS

Estepona
Algeciras

KM
163

Marbella
Malaga

Los Flamingos

18^{+9}

Los Flamingos Golf Club

Tel: 952 889 163 Fax: 952 889 102

Ctra. de Cadiz, N340 Km.166
29679 Benahavis, Malaga

info@flamingos-golf.com
www.flamingos-golf.com

METRES	PAR	CV	SLOPE
5883	72	70.6	128
5619	71	69.3	125
4993	71	71.2	127

Established, in a short space of time, as one of the most prestigious courses on the coast. It has already hosted The European Seniors Match-Play Championships three times. A short 9-hole course has also recently been added to the many facilities on offer.

Features:
Hotel
Driving Range
Gym
Jacuzzi
Lockers

Designer:
Antonio Garcia
 Garrido

Opened:
2001

Photo: Miguel Toro

Courtesy Costa del Sol Tourist Board www.visitcostadelsol.com

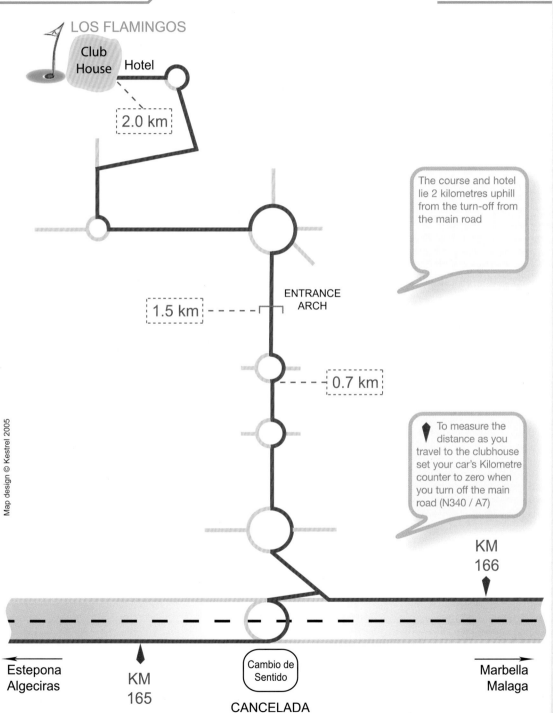

Los Almendros

MAP **12**

Los Almendros Golf Club

Tel: 952 113 327   Fax: 952 113 551

Ctra. de Genalquacil Km. 3
29680 Estepona, Malaga

info@losalmendrosgolf.com
www.losalmendrosgolf.com

Features:
Driving Range
Lessons
Golf School
Club Rental

Designer:
Bartolomé Benitez

Opened:
1999

A pitch and putt course, set in a valley of almond trees with magnificent views of the countryside from the restaurant.

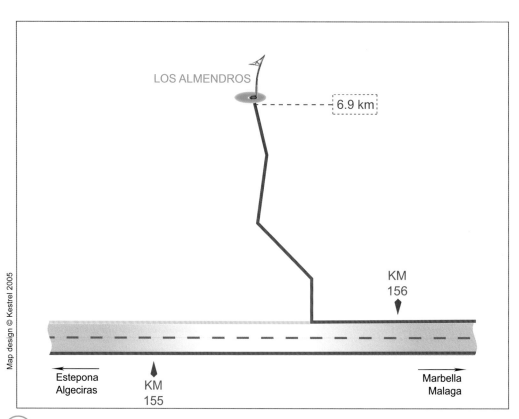

LOS ALMENDROS

6.9 km

KM
156

Map design © Kestrel 2005

Estepona
Algeciras

KM
155

Marbella
Malaga

El Paraiso Golf Club

Tel: 952 883 835 Fax: 952 885 827

Urb. El Paraiso, N340 Km.167
29680 Estepona, Malaga

info@elparaisogolfclub.com
www.elparaisogolfclub.com

METRES	PAR	CV	SLOPE
6131	72	72.5	134
5912	71	71.5	130
4998	71	71.2	119

El Paraiso Golf is a traditional 'British' club, with an international membership, professionally managed and owned by the members. Visitors are welcome to this very friendly club where special competitions are often arranged.

Features:
Hotel
Driving Range
Storage
Club Rental

Designer:
Gary Player

Opened:
1974

Courtesy El Paraiso Golf

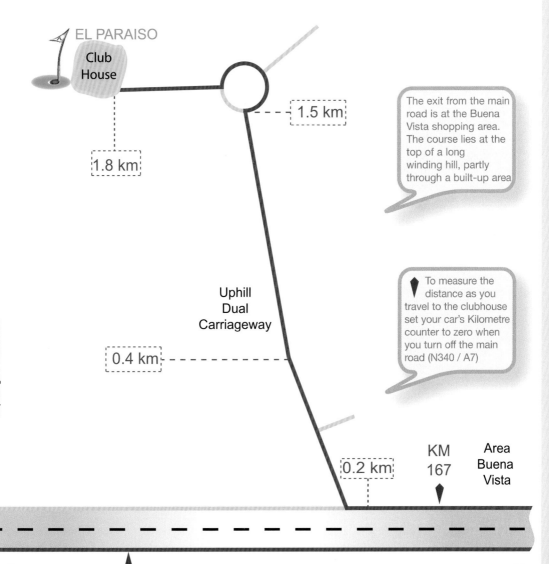

El Campanario

9 holes

MAP **14**

El Campanario Golf

Tel: 660 722 025

Ctra. de Cadiz, (N340) Km. 168
29680 Estepona, Malaga

Features:
Driving Range
Lessons
Storage
Dressing Room

Designer:

Opened:

Suitable for all levels of player, set in pleasant surroundings of lakes and countryside vegetation.

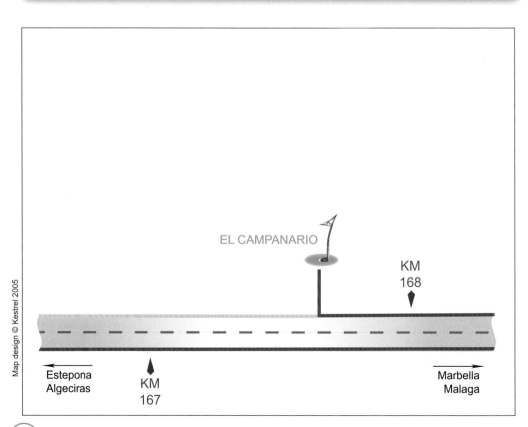

EL CAMPANARIO

KM
168

Map design © Kestrel 2005

Estepona
Algeciras

KM
167

Marbella
Malaga

Atalaya Park

Atalaya Park Golf Hotel & Resort

Tel: 952 882 812   Fax: 952 887 897

Ctra. Benahavis Km. 0.7
29688 Estepona, Malaga

atalayagolf@selected-hotels.com
www.atalaya-golf.com

ATALAYA OLD

METRES	PAR	CV	SLOPE
6142	72	71.0	133
5856	72	70.8	135
5178	72	72.7	128

ATALAYA NEW

METRES	PAR	CV	SLOPE
5325	67	68.1	125
5217	67	67.7	124
4510	67	67.8	120

Features:
Hotel
Driving Range
Lockers
Golf School

Designers:
Bernhard Von
   Limburger
P. Krings

Opened:
Old 1968
New 1991

The Atalaya Park Golf complex is one of the most popular golfing venues on the Coast. It is the official headquarters of the PGA of Europe which covers 29 countries and 7500 professionals. The teaching side is well covered and many visit this hotel / course complex on a regular basis for lessons and tuition.

Courtesy Junta de Andalucia

To
Monte Mayor Golf
Marbella Club GR

A short drive from the turn-off from the dual carriageway, after negotiating the Benahavis *cambio de sentido*

ATALAYA PARK

Club
House

0.9 km

To measure the distance as you travel to the clubhouse set your car's Kilometre counter to zero when you turn off the main road (N340 / A7)

MA547
to Benahavis

Map design © Kestrel 2005

KM
Marbella 170
Arch

Estepona
Algeciras

KM
169

Cambio de
Sentido

Marbella
Malaga

BENAHAVIS

Marbella Club Golf Resort

Tel: 952 889 101   Fax: 952 889 102

Ctra. de Benahavis Km 3.7
29679 Benahavis, Malaga

reserv.golf@marbellaclub.com
www.marbellaclub.com

METRES	PAR	CV	SLOPE
6279	73	74.1	129
5891	73		
5437	73		
5050	73		

Built in the hills of Benahavis, this magnificent course is part of the Marbella Club/Puente Romano Hotel group and, along with villa owners, gives preferred tee-times. However, visitors are welcome. The front nine includes three consecutive par-5 holes.

Features:
Driving Range
Lockers
Storage

Designer:
Dave Thomas

Opened:
1999

Photo: Miguel Toro   Courtesy Costa del Sol Tourist Board www.visitcostadelsol.com

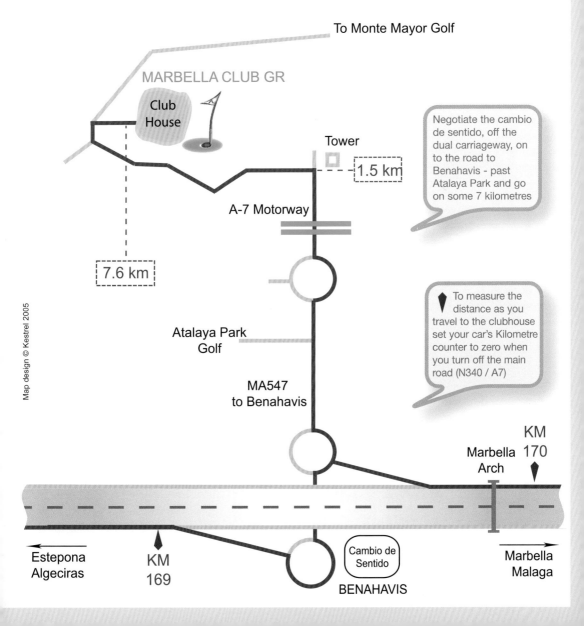

Monte Mayor

Monte Mayor Golf & Country Club

Tel: 952 937 111   Fax: 952 937 112

Avda. Monte mayor,
29679 Benahavis, Malaga

reservations@montemayorgolf.com
www.montemayorgolf.com

METRES	PAR	CV	SLOPE
5652	71	70.3	136
5354	71	68.6	132
4800	71	71.3	124
4800	71	71.3	124

Monte Mayor is, without doubt, a spectacular golf course, set in a high mountain valley - each hole surprises the first-time visitor. The designer's philosophy was: 'Why move the earth when the fairway should follow the natural contours?'

Features:
All buggies equipped with GPS hand-held units. Green fee includes buggy for 2

Designer:
Jose Gancedo Gomez

Opened:
1989

Photo: José Hidalgo

Courtesy Costa del Sol Tourist Board www.visitcostadelsol.com

MONTE MAYOR

Club
House

15.0 km

Marbella Club GR

Tower

1.5 km

Negotiate the cambio
de sentido, off the dual
carriageway, on to the
road to Benahavis -
past Atalaya Park and
Marbella club and go
on some 15 kilometres

A-7 Motorway

7.6 km

Atalaya Park
Golf

To measure the
distance as you
travel to the clubhouse
set your car's Kilometre
counter to zero when
you turn off the main
road (N340 / A7)

MA547
to Benahavis

KM
170

Marbella
Arch

Map design © Kestrel 2005

Estepona
Algeciras

KM
169

Cambio de
Sentido

BENAHAVIS

Marbella
Malaga

Guadalmina

Guadalmina Golf Club
Tel: 952 886 522   Fax: 952 883 483
Urb. Guadalmina Alta
29678 San Pedro, Marbella Malaga
info@guadalminagolf.org
www.guadalminagolf.org

SOUTH

METRES	PAR	CV	SLOPE
6021	71	73.6	140
5874	71	71.8	137
5173	71	75.1	137
5108	71	72.8	132

NORTH

METRES	PAR	CV	SLOPE
5768	72	70.2	126
5644	72	69.8	124
5063	72	71.7	125
4820	72	70.3	120

Features:
Hotel
Driving Range
Sauna, Pool
Tennis
Paddle Tennis
Lockers / Storage

Designers:
Sth - Javier Arana
Nth - Folco Nardi

Opened:
South 1959
North 1973

The second oldest golf club on the Costa del Sol, Guadalmina opened in 1959 as a nine-hole course (South). It was extended to 18 holes in the late 60's. The North course was opened in 1973. Guadalmina has hosted the PGA European Tour Qualifying School several times.

Photo: José Hidalgo

Courtesy Costa del Sol Tourist Board www.visitcostadelsol.com

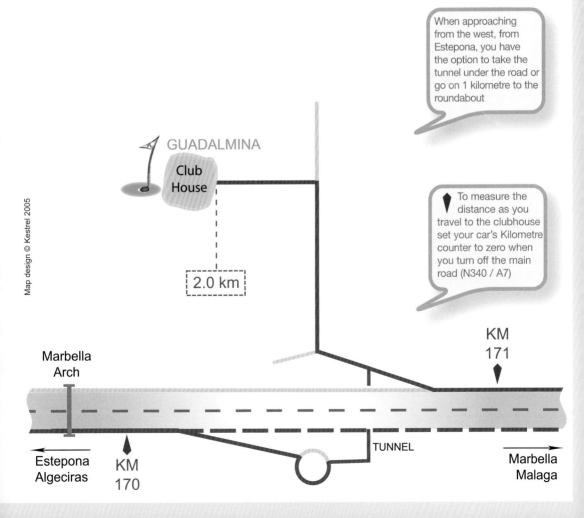

GOLF COURSES	MAP
La Quinta	19
Los Arqueros	20
La Zagaleta	21
Aloha	22
Las Brisas	23
Los Naranjos	24
La Dama de Noche	25
Monte Paraiso	26

Jose Hidalgo

Los Naranjos Golf Club

AREA 3 The Area covers the courses just to the west of Marbella. At the entrance to Marbella, west-side, and forming part of "Golf Valley", are Aloha, Las Brisas, and Los Naranjos and the flood-lit course of La Dama de Noche. La Quinta lies near by the start of the road from the Coast up to Ronda and a few kilometres inland along the Ronda road are Los Arqueros and La Zagaleta. Main population centre is Marbella, with access to the Old Quarter and Orange Square (Plaza de los Naranjos) either through the town centre or off the bypass. San Pedro and the fashionable marina of Puerto Banus are nearby, together with the road inland leading to the historic and cultural town of Ronda a few hours drive away. Puerto Banus and Marbella offer a wide selection of restaurants, shopping, cultural activities and night-life

Cartoon : ELVON

CAMPO DE GOLF

...We'll get you to the tee on time !

Villa ESPAÑA

A Great Way To Buy!

Dear Client,

This is really big! After 15 years involved in the real estate business in Spain I can say with complete conviction that Polaris World is one of the most impressive investment opportunities I've ever come across.

Located in the Murcia region, inland from the internationally renowned La Manga golfing resort, Polaris World epitomises the future of residential-tourism in Spain. This newly flourishing area offers the best of Mediterranean living without the high-density building that besets other parts of the Spanish coastline.

Security is a major consideration for anyone contemplating a move away from familiar surroundings, especially to another country, and it certainly is a priority at Polaris World. All Polaris World resorts feature passive and active security systems reinforced by fully enclosed perimeters controlled by 24-hour security personnel, which means the residential complexes are open, family-orientated, relaxing and comfortable. In short, pure pleasure in tranquil, safe and beautifully landscaped surroundings. (Associate company Polaris Garden has more than 35,000 trees ready to be planted in the resorts, including elegant palm trees and 100-year-old olive trees.)

Access can also be compared favourably with communications services in more established areas such as the Costa del Sol. Offering 20 daily flights from abroad, Alicante and Murcia international airports are just 45 and 10 minutes, respectively, from the most distant Polaris World resort, and Spain's massively upgraded motorway network provides quick and efficient links with other provincial capitals.

Not that residents have to leave home, however, because at the heart of each resort is a "town centre" - a traditional style village with all the essential ingredients for a memorable holiday or longer-term stay: supermarkets, restaurants, pubs, swimming pools, sports clubs, etc. And then there's the golf. Polaris World employs the services of Jack Nicklaus's design company to create many of its courses - and they don't come any better or more prestigious than that.

So what does all this mean for the discerning investor? Essentially it means you will be a major player in the first chapter of a guaranteed success story. Polaris World's Murcia resorts are the future of expatriate living in Spain, and you have a superb chance of being in at the start. Villa España will be pleased to give you more information about this exceptional investment opportunity, and set you on the path to lucrative rewards at Polaris World. Contact us at our Manchester branch or any of our Costa del Sol offices.

"After 15 years involved in real estate in Spain I can say with complete conviction that Polaris World is one of the most impressive investment opportunities I've ever come across."

Phillip Nuttall - Director, Villa España

For more information call UK freephone 0800-107 7976 or visit any of our Costa del Sol branches.

www.villaspain.com

www.villaspain.com

La Quinta Golf & Country Club

Tel: 952 762 390   Fax: 952 762 399

Urb. La Quinta Golf, 29660
Nueva Andalucia, Marbella, Malaga

reservas@laquintagolf.com
www.laquintagolf.com

Features:
Hotel
Driving Range
Fitness Centre
Squash, Pool
Sauna
Lockers / Storage

Designers:
Antonio Garcia
Manuel Piñero

Opened:
1989

Apart from the 27 holes making up La Quinta Golf & Country Club there is a large driving range with a capacity for 100 golfers. Three times world champion Manuel Piñero, also of Ryder Cup fame, runs the golf academy on site.

LA QUINTA A + B

METRES	PAR	CV	SLOPE
5798	72	72.3	141
5540	72	71.1	141
4823	72	71.6	129

LA QUINTA B + C

METRES	PAR	CV	SLOPE
5705	72	71.4	136
5489	72	70.4	135
4842	72	72.1	129

LA QUINTA C + A

METRES	PAR	CV	SLOPE
5737	72	71.4	133
5457	72	70.0	134
4657	72	70.5	126

Photo: José Hidalgo   Courtesy Costa del Sol Tourist Board www.visitcostadelsol.com

LA QUINTA

Club House

1.8 km

A7 Motorway

Road to Ronda

Turn off the main road at the traffic lights just outside San Pedro and take the Ronda road for almost 2 kilometres

1.6 km

Petrol

To measure the distance as you travel to the clubhouse set your car's Kilometre counter to zero when you turn off the main road (N340 / A7)

Road to Ronda

KM 173

Estepona
Algeciras

KM 172

Marbella
Malaga

Los Arqueros

Los Arqueros Golf & Country Club

Tel: 952 784 600   Fax: 952 786 707

Apdo. 110, Ctra. de Ronda Km. s/n
29670 San Pedro de Alcantara, Malaga

admin.losarquerosgolf@es.taylorwoodrow.com
www.taylorwoodrow.com

METRES	PAR	CV	SLOPE
5729	71	70.7	132
5306	71	68.3	129
4819	71	70.5	129

Set amongst the Ronda hills, Los Arqueros is just a short drive from San Pedro and the first on the coast designed by Ryder Cup Captain Seve Ballesteros. Exceptional views are part of the Los Arqueros experience - The nearby Rio Verde supplies the three lakes on course.

Features:
Driving Range
Gym
Sauna
Tennis,
Squash
Lockers

Designer:
Seve Ballesteros

Opened:
1991

Photo: José Hidalgo

Courtesy Costa del Sol Tourist Board www.visitcostadelsol.com

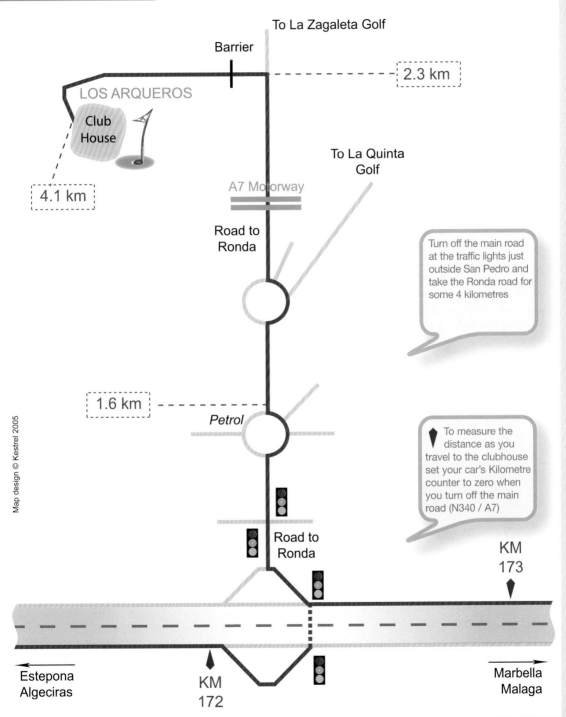

La Zagaleta Country Club
Tel: 952 855 453   Fax: 952 855 419
Ctra. Ronda Km. 11
29679 Benahavis, Malaga
zagaleta@golf-andalucia.net
www.zagaleta.com

METRES	PAR	CV	SLOPE
6039	72	71.8	132
5709	72	70.3	132
4883	72	73.2	126
4760	72	70.8	121

This very exclusive golf club is situated on the Ronda Road in the fabulous former estate of the Saudi magnate Adnan Kashogui. The course is located in a protected nature reserve.

Features:
Driving Range,
Caddies
Lockers
Storage

Designer:
Bradford Benz

Opened:
1994

Photo: Miguel Toro
Courtesy Costa del Sol Tourist Board www.visitcostadelsol.com

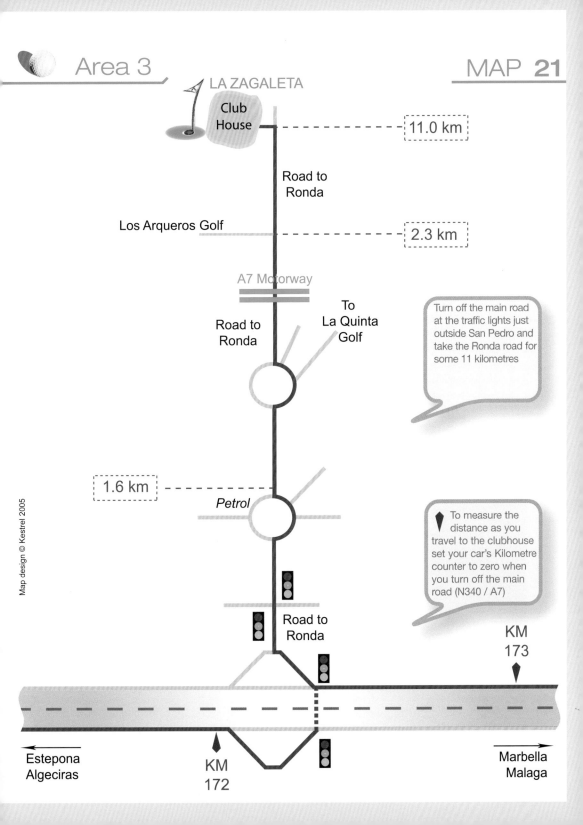

Aloha

Aloha Golf Club

Tel: 952 812 388   Fax: 952 812 389

Urb. Aloha Golf, 29660
Nueva Andalucia, Marbella, Malaga

office@clubdegolfaloha.com
www.clubdegolfalhoa.com

METRES	PAR	CV	SLOPE
6293	72	73.5	140
6007	72	71.9	137
5650	72	76.1	132
5254	72	73.4	129

Part of the now famous Golf Valley, Aloha Golf is a private club but allows visitors. The course is built on land originally known as the 'Finca del Angel'. Aloha is just eight km. from Marbella centre and Puerto Banus is close by.

Features:
Driving Range
Pool, Sauna
Lockers

Designer:
Javier Arana

Opened:
1975

Photo: José Hidalgo

Courtesy Costa del Sol Tourist Board www.visitcostadelsol.com

ALOHA

Club
House

To Los Naranjos Golf
Las Brisas Golf

1.8 km

Turn off the bypass on
the west side of
Marbella at the tunnel
and travel just under
2 kilometres on the
road to Istan, into the
heart of the Golf Valley

Aloha College

0.8 km

To measure the
distance as you
travel to the clubhouse
set your car's Kilometre
counter to zero when
you turn off the main
road (N340 / A7)

Driving
Range

BRIDGE

Map design © Kestrel 2005

0.3 km

MA427
to Istan

KM
177

TUNNEL

Estepona
Algeciras

KM
176

Marbella
Malaga

Las Brisas

Royal Las Brisas Golf Club

Tel: 952 810 875   Fax: 952 815 324

Apdo. de Correos 147
29660 Marbella, Malaga

secretaria@lasbrisasgolf.com
www.lasbrisasgolf.com

METRES	PAR	CV	SLOPE
6130	72	72.4	126
5866	72	70.9	125
5593	72	71.0	137
5069	72	71.5	126

Renowned as one of the top courses in Spain. Restricted visitors' tee-times are available from the caddy-master in the afternoons. It has hosted the Spanish Open on three occasions and the World Cup twice. Royal Las Brisas is part of the famous 'Golf Valley'.

Features:
Hotel
Driving Range
Sauna
Caddies
Lockers / Storage

Designer:
Robert Trent
Jones Snr

Opened:
1968

Photo: José Hidalgo

Courtesy Costa del Sol Tourist Board www.visitcostadelsol.com

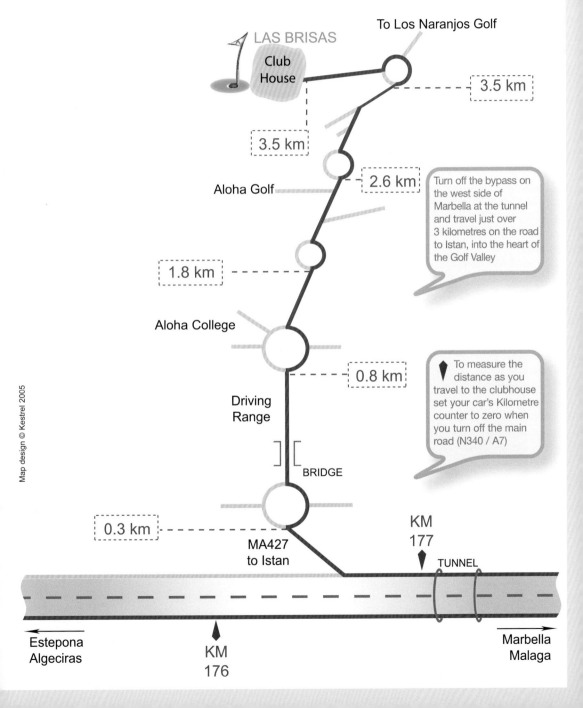

Los Naranjos

Los Naranjos Golf Club
Tel: 952 815 206   Fax: 952 812 428
Nueva Andalucia
29660 Marbella, Malaga
teetimes@losnaranjos.com
www.losnaranjos.com

METRES	PAR	CV	SLOPE
6457	72	74.1	130
6038	72	71.9	129
5143	72	71.8	124

A course of two different halves. The front nine has rolling, wide fairways but the back nine is much tighter having been built in the middle of an orange grove. It's like playing two separate courses. A very impressive clubhouse overlooks the 18th green.

Features:
Driving Range
Sauna
Caddies
Lockers
Storage

Designer:
Robert Trent
  Jones Snr

Opened:
1977

Photo: José Hidalgo

Courtesy Costa del Sol Tourist Board www.visitcostadelsol.com

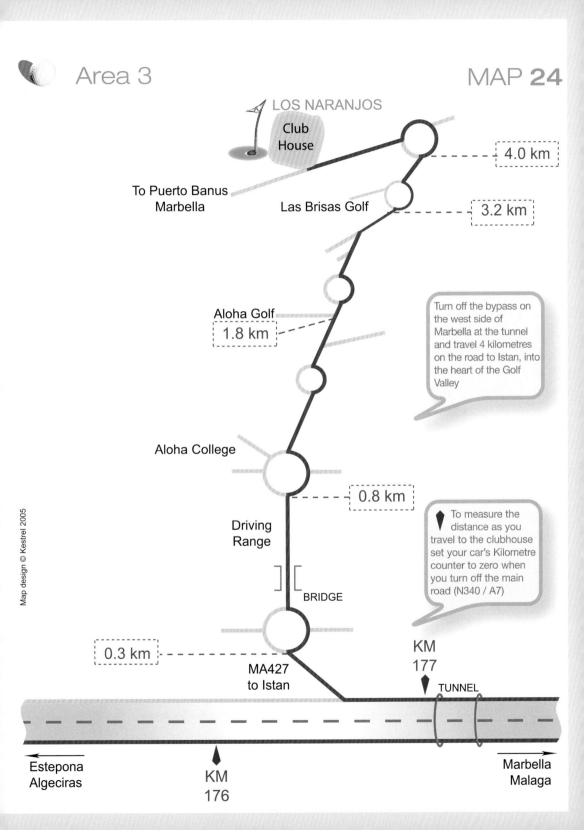

La Dama de Noche Golf Club

Tel: 952 818 150 Fax: 952 818 413

Camino del Angel s/n, Rio Verde
29660 Nueva Andalucia-Marbella, Malaga

reservas@golfdamadenoche.com
www.golfdamadenoche.com

Features:
Floodlit
Buggies
Club Rental

Designer:
Enrique Canales

Opened:
1991

This golf-course is unique in that it is floodlit and can be played at night as well as by day. A minimum of 10 golfers is required after dark and must be booked in advance. The course was the venue for the world record attempt by David Steele playing 24 hours non-stop.

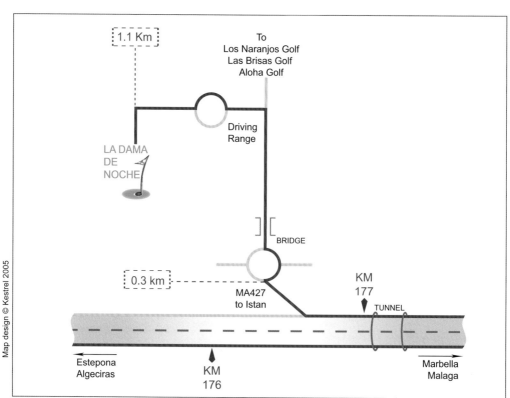

Location, location, ~~location~~ *currency*

Fluctuating exchange rates could put your dreams out of reach

To minimise the risk of paying more when **buying** or **selling** abroad, call us now and speak to one of our expert advisers or visit www.hifx.co.uk/abroad

In addition we can protect you from currency risk and if you send regular payments abroad (for a mortgage or pension transfer) we can fix an exchange rate for up to 2 years, establish a direct debit with your UK bank and send the currency abroad for no charge.

UK Head Office: +44(0)1753 859159
Spanish Office: 952 587 507

info@hifx.co.uk

Monte Paraiso Golf

Tel: 952 828 781   Fax: 952 822 714

Camino de Camojan s/n
29660 Marbella, Malaga

monteparaisogolf@monteparaisogolf.com
www.monteparaisogolf.com

Features:
Driving Range
Lessons
Club Rental

Designer:
Begoña Castillo
 Velasco

Opened:

Located a few minutes from the centre of Marbella, the course has beautiful sea-views and many amentities.

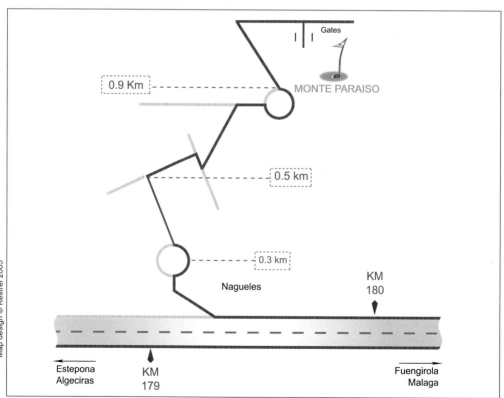

look around

to see how much we've changed

www.visitcostadelsol.com

Come to see us

because we have much more,

come to the Costa del Sol.

COSTA DEL SOL
PATRONATO DE TURISMO

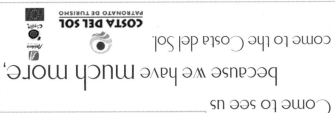

Come and enjoy, our traditions,
history, food,
hospitality... and,
of course, our climate.

Because we have a lot of art,
because we've modernised,
because we have a lot to offer:
we want to show you our past, present... and future.

TAMAYA·J. VALEROB

crown
CAR HIRE

Invaral S.A. is an all-Spanish company with their head office in Malaga and the owner of Crown car hire.

The company head office is situated at Malaga international airport. Crown car hire owns premises with a total 400sm of office and garage space, wich houses all the necessary installations suchs as customer reception area and the most modern and up to date reservations and customer care centre.

Inside the airport building the Crown car hire desk has six computer terminals, wich can absorb in excess of 100 clients per hour.

the development

Crown car hire was founded in March 1995 and since then established itself as the largest privately owned car rental company in Andalusia today, with a total of 8.000 vehicles on its fleet.

the fleet

Crown car hire offers you the most modern fleet with all new cars from 15 different manufacturers and over 38 models to choose from, the fleet is renewed continuously and the average age of the cars are six months.

The best drive in golf

CROWN CAR HIRE HEAD OFFICE

Málaga airport
Head office
Courtesy bus service. Avda. García. Morato, 34
29004 MALAGA
Tel. 952 176 486 - Fax: 952 246 719
Emergency: 609 026 985

Málaga airport
Desk in Terminal building ✈
29004 MALAGA
Tel. 952 048 490 - Fax: 952 048 488

BRANCH OFFICES IN ANDALUCIA

Granada
Hotel San Antón
C/ San Antón, s/n.
18005 GRANADA
Tel./FAX.: 958 255 399
Móvil: 669 470 784

Almuñecar
Paseo San Cristóbal, 7. Edf. Vista Azul
18690 ALMUÑECAR
Tel. 958 880 240 - Fax: 958 633 396
Móvil: 696 902 193

Nerja
C/ Chaparil, 28. Edf. Algarrobo
29780 NERJA
Tel. 952 527 159 - Fax: 952 523 317
Móvil: 630 026 633

Torremolinos
C/ Las Mercedes, 17.
29620 TORREMOLINOS
Tel. 952 386 344 - Fax: 952 386 344
Móvil: 639 479 050

Torremolinos II (Montemar)
Crown Safari Tours & Incentives
Ctra. Carlota Alessandri, 264
Tel.: 95 205 70 79 - Fax: 95 205 81 06
Móvil: 630 98 48 69

Fuengirola
C/ Lamo de Espinosa, Edif. PYR, local 8
FUENGIROLA
Tel./Fax: 952 666 328
Móvil: 619 032 405

Marbella - Puerto Banus
C/ Naciones Unidas 62, C. C. Cristamar-Bajo
29600 MARBELLA
Tel. 952 819 000 - Fax: 952 810 103
Móvil: 629 632 321 - 679 975 926

Sotogrande - Gibraltar
C/ Sierra Bermeja s/n ✈
11310 GUADIARO
Tel. 956 695 315 - Fax: 956 794 224
Móvil: 629 678 386

Chiclana - Frontera
C.C. Altamar, local 6. Novo Sancti Petri
11130 CHICLANA
Tel. 956 492 114 - Fax: 956 492 115
Móvil: 699 943 569

Cádiz
Estación Marítima
11006 CADIZ
Tel. 956 221 038 - Fax: 956 492 115
Móvil: 699 943 569

Jerez de la Frontera
Ctra. Nacional IV, Km 634.1 ✈
11407 JEREZ
Tel. 956 318 035 - Fax: 956 318 036
Móvil: 699 943 568

Rota
Plaza del Triunfo,1
11520 ROTA
Tel. 956 843 038 - Fax: 956 843 038
Móvil: 699 943 007

Sevilla Airport
Desk in Terminal. ✈
SEVILLA
Tel. 954 516 808 - Fax: 954 514 853
Móvil: 699 943 627

Sevilla
Avda. Kansas City. Núcleo San Estanislao, 9
41007 SEVILLA
Tel. 954 980 214 - Fax: 954 980 213
Móvil: 699 943 627

Huelva
C.C. de Islantilla, local B4
21410 Islantilla-Isla Cristina HUELVA
Tel. 959 646 075 - Fax: 959 646 049
Móvil: 619 038 947

crown
CAR HIRE

GOLF COURSES	MAP
Rio Real	27
Santa Clara	28
Marbella Golf CC	29
El Soto	30
Greenlife	31
Santa Maria	32
Artola	33
Cabopino	34

Cabopino Golf Marbella

AREA 4 The Area lies between Marbella to the west and Fuengirola to the east. A few kilometres from the east-side of Marbella are Rio Real, Santa Clara, Marbella Golf & Country Club and Santa Maria. A few kilometres more, after Calahonda, is Cabopino, close to the yacht-marina. Main population centre is Marbella, with access to the port area, and to the Old Quarter and Orange Square (Plaza de los Naranjos) off the bypass. Stretching along the beach side of the main road as it leaves Marbella are pine-groves, and in places sand-dunes until the road reaches the small marina of Cabopino. Most of the courses now are set within built-up areas, except Cabopino. Calahonda offers a selection of bars, cafes and restaurants , mostly of an international, rather than a local style and Fuengirola is a main town with shopping, port/marina, restaurants and night-life.

...We'll get you
to the tee
on time !

Rio Real Golf

Tel: 952 765 733 Fax: 952 772 140

Urb. Golf Rio Real, N340 Km.185
29600 Marbella, Malaga

reservas@rioreal.com
www.rioreal.com

METRES	PAR	CV	SLOPE
6166	72	72.1	132
6098	72	71.4	129
5321	72	73.6	128

Named after the river creek which meanders through the course to the Mediterranean only a short distance away. The course is now 40 years old and is well-loved by the locals from Marbella just three kilometres to the west.

Features:
Hotel
Lockers
Storage

Designer:
Javier Arana

Opened:
1965

Courtesy Junta de Andalucia

1.7 km

RIO REAL

Hotel
Incosol

Club
House

Exit the main road
and travel just under
2 kilometres to the
course

To measure the
distance as you
travel to the clubhouse
set your car's Kilometre
counter to zero when
you turn off the main
road (N340 / A7)

KM
186

Map design © Kestrel 2005

Marbella
Algeciras

KM
185

Cambio de
Sentido

Fuengirola
Malaga

TORRE REAL

Santa Clara

Santa Clara Golf Club

Tel: 952 850 111   Fax: 952 850 288

Ctra. de Cadiz, N340 Km. 187.5
29600 Marbella, Malaga

reservas@santaclara-golf.com
www.gruposantaclara.com

METRES	PAR	CV	SLOPE
5940	71		126
5558	71		123
5245	72		123
4856	72		120

The 360 acre estate also houses many fine villas and apartments. All greens are to USGA standard and the first-class service given to visitors is second to none in Spain.

Features:
Driving Range
Lockers
Storage

Designer:
Enrique Canales
  Busquet

Opened:
2000

Photo: Miguel Toro

Courtesy Costa del Sol Tourist Board www.visitcostadelsol.com

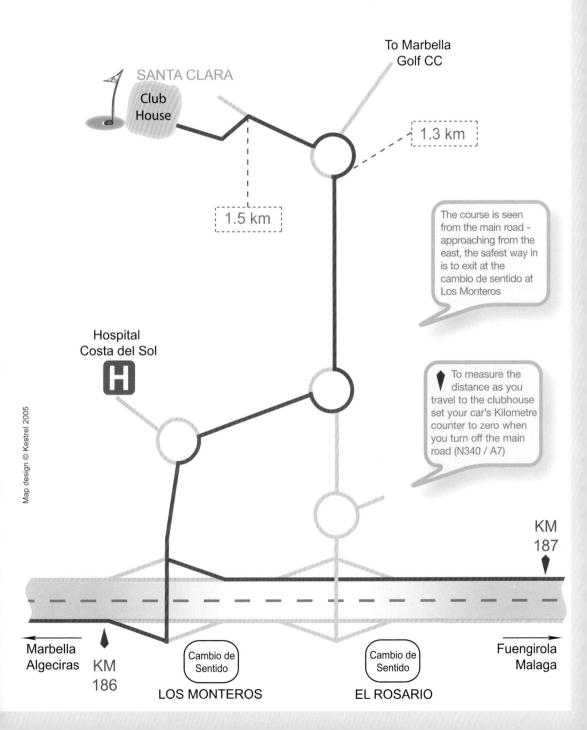

To Marbella
Golf CC

SANTA CLARA

Club
House

1.3 km

1.5 km

The course is seen
from the main road -
approaching from the
east, the safest way in
is to exit at the
cambio de sentido at
Los Monteros

Hospital
Costa del Sol

H

To measure the
distance as you
travel to the clubhouse
set your car's Kilometre
counter to zero when
you turn off the main
road (N340 / A7)

KM
187

Map design © Kestrel 2005

KM
186

Marbella
Algeciras

Cambio de
Sentido

Cambio de
Sentido

Fuengirola
Malaga

LOS MONTEROS

EL ROSARIO

Marbella Golf & Country Club

Tel: 952 830 500 Fax: 952 834 353

Ctra. de Cadiz Km 188
29600 Marbella, Malaga

reserv.golf@marbellaclub.com
www.marbellagolfcc.com

METRES	PAR	CV	SLOPE
5953	72	71.4	129
5602	72	69.5	127
5033	72	72.2	124
4777	72	69.6	118

Another great golf-course designed by 'The Master' Robert Trent Jones Snr. Some rough can be awkward but fairways are generous as are the the greens. A large clubhouse enables players to relax after a game and use the wonderful facilities on offer.

Features:
Driving Range
Golf School
Jacuzzi
Sauna, Gym
Lockers
Storage

Designer:
Robert Trent
Jones Snr

Opened:
1994

Photo: Miguel Toro

Courtesy Costa del Sol Tourist Board www.visitcostadelsol.com

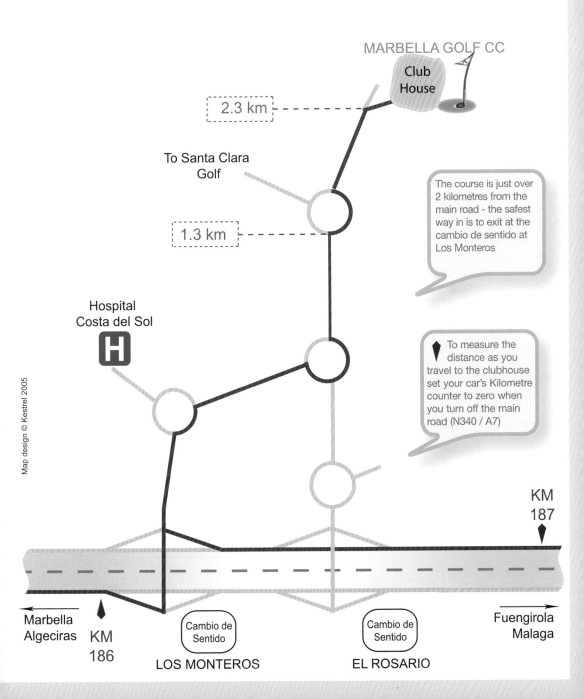

El Soto

MAP **30**

El Soto de Marbella Golf Club

Tel: 952 852 116   Fax: 952 852 120

Urb. El Soto ,Elviria- La Mairena km 3
29610 Ojen, Malaga

caddy-master@elsotoclubdegolf.com
www.elsotoclubdegolf.com

Features:
Driving Range
Lockers
Club Rental
Dressing Room

Designer:
Manuel Piñero
(modified)

Opened:
2004

Suitable to improve short play and for beginners taking first steps.

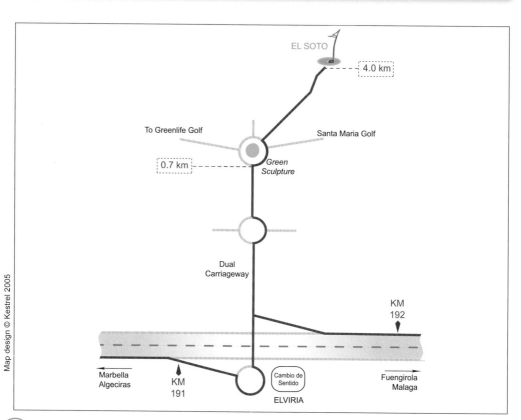

Map design © Kestrel 2005

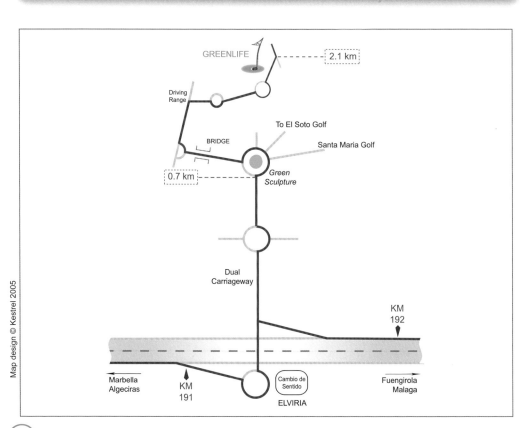

Greenlife Golf Club

Tel: 952 839 142   Fax: 952 839 082

Urb. Elviria Hills,Avda de las Cumbres s/n
29600 Marbella, Malaga

golf@greenlife-estates.es
www.greenlife-estates.es

Features:
Driving Range
Lockers
Golf School
Lessons

Designer:

Opened:

A short distance from Marbella and enjoyable at all levels playing in spectacular wooded scenery with a fine clubhouse overlooking the lake.

GREENLIFE

2.1 km

Driving
Range

BRIDGE

To El Soto Golf

Santa Maria Golf

0.7 km

*Green
Sculpture*

Dual
Carriageway

KM
192

Marbella
Algeciras

KM
191

Cambio de
Sentido

Fuengirola
Malaga

ELVIRIA

Map design © Kestrel 2005

Santa Maria

Santa Maria Golf & Country Club

Tel: 952 831 036   Fax: 952 834 797

Urb. Elviria, N340 Km.192
29600 Marbella, Malaga

caddy-master@santamariagolfclub.com
www.santamariagolfclub.com

METRES	PAR	CV	SLOPE
5586	70	68.2	114
5325	70	67.1	120
4657	70	58.2	113

Only nine holes were open until 1996 when the technical staff at Santa Maria put their heads together and produced the back nine – an amazing feat. A further 18 holes is planned with Dave Thomas as the architect. The 19th century clubhouse gives this complex an air of serenity.

Features:
Lockers / Storage
Lawn Bowls
Tennis
Sauna

Designers:
Antonio Garcia
  Garrido &
Technical Staff at
Club
Opened:
1991/1996

Courtesy Junta de Andalucia

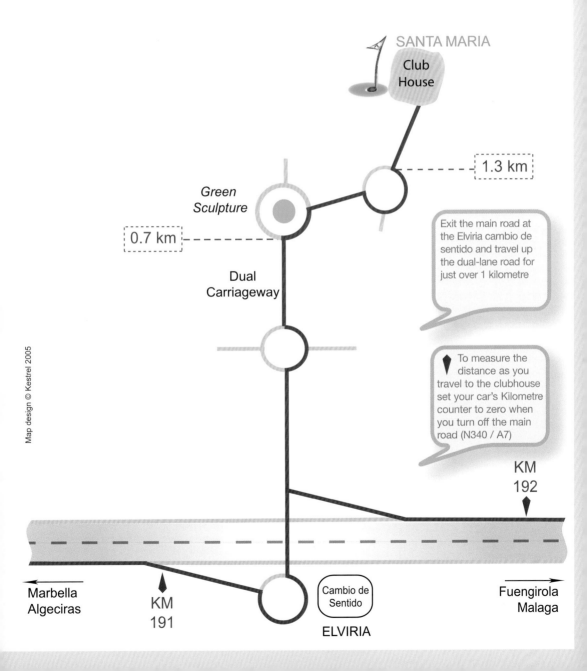

Artola

MAP **33**

Hotel Artola Golf

Tel: 952 831 390 Fax: 952 830 450

Ctra. de Cadiz, (N340) Km. 194
29600 Marbella, Malaga

Features:
Driving Range
Club Rental
Storage
Lessons

Designer:
Gorge Rein

Opened:
1964

Surrounded by pine-trees, the course stretches from the road down to the sea with the total distance of all the holes just 700m.

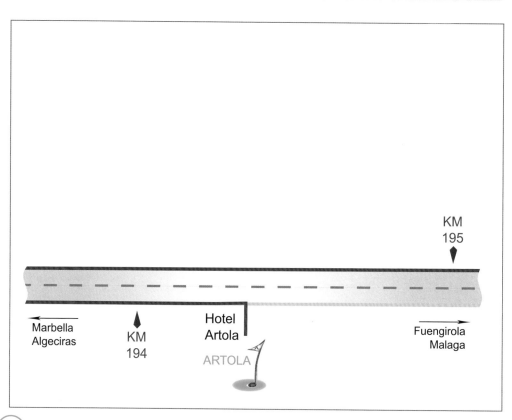

Cabopino

Cabopino Golf Marbella

Tel: 952 850 282   Fax: 952 837 277

Artola Alta s/n, Ap. 2119
29600 Marbella, Malaga

reservas@cabopinogolf.com
www.cabopinogolf.com

METRES	PAR	CV	SLOPE
5417	71	68.0	121
4640	71	69.9	121

A 'buggies are obligatory' rule but most golfers are happy about that! This modern course has several interesting holes especially the third which drops dramatically from the tee to the green. The views over the Mediterranean are spectacular.

Features:
Driving Range
Club Repair
Lockers

Designer:
Juan Ligues
 Creus

Opened:
2000

Photo: Cabopino Golf

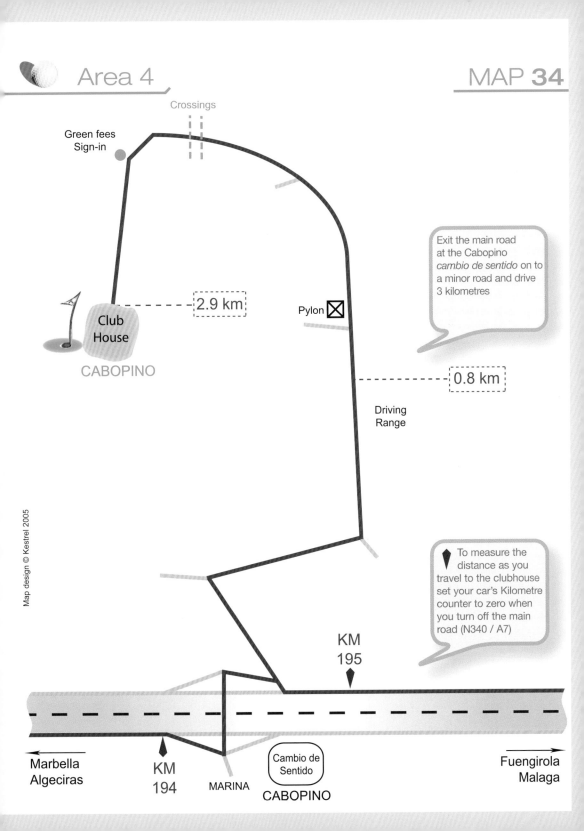

GOLF COURSES	MAP
La Siesta	35
Miraflores	36
La Noria	37
La Cala	38
Santana	39
Mijas	40

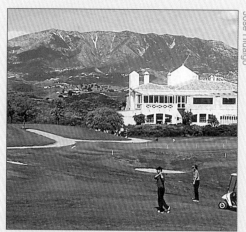

Jose Hidalgo

Miraflores Golf Club

AREA 5 The Area lies between Marbella to the west and Fuengirola to the east and just before the Golf Valley around La Cala and Mijas is Miraflores. A little inland on the road towards La Cala is Santana Golf. The courses are mostly in a rural setting, but with urbanisations growing up around them. Main population centre is Fuengirola, a main town with shopping, port/marina, restaurants and night-life but the many urbanisations and shopping centres along the main road include Miraflores, Calahonda and La Cala de Mijas, offering a wide selection of bars, cafes and restaurants. Mijas, a few kilometres inland, is a traditional Andalusian "white village" and offers a wide range of national and international bars, cafes and restaurants. The sea side of the road is well-known for its pine groves growing down to the undeveloped parts of the beaches.

Cartoon : EVON

CAMPO DE GOLF

...We'll get you to the tee on time !

La Siesta

MAP **35**

9 holes La Siesta

La Siesta Golf

Tel: 952 933 362   Fax: 952 933 352

Urb. Sitio de Calahonda, C/ Jose de Orbaneja
29650 Mijas Costa, Malaga

Lasiestagolf@mixmail.com
www.geocities.com/lasiestagolf

Features:
Driving Range
Lockers
Sauna
Lessons

Designer:
Enrique Busquet

Opened:
1990

The round is varied and ideal for short play, with fine views to the Mediterranean.

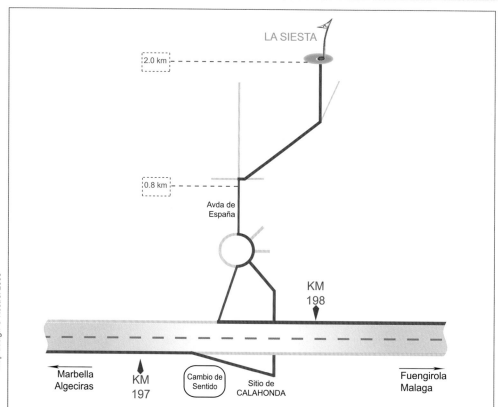

Map design © Kestrel 2005

COLISEUM
BAR & GRILL
For All the Family

open all day for
Breakfast, Lunch and Dinner

Golfers Breakfast from 3.25€
Our famous Sunday Roast only 9.99€

- Reservations: 952 494 641

28 Bulevard de La Cala, La Cala de Mijas

Restaurante "Santana Bar"

Santana Golf & Country Club
Ctra. La Cala-Entrerríos, s/n - Valle del Golf de Mijas
29649 Mijas Costa - Málaga - España
www.santanagolf.com

Miraflores Golf Club
Tel: 952 931 960   Fax: 952 931 942
Ctra. de Cadiz N340 Km.199
29647 Mijas Costa, Malaga
miraflores@computronx.com

METRES	PAR	CV	SLOPE
5113	71		
4988	71	65.8	123
4419	71	67.6	119

The purpose-built floodlit two-story driving range, with video analysis is nearby the course, itself nestling in the hills of Mijas Costa overlooking the Mediterranean. Elevated greens and undulating fairways could require some tough walking so a buggy may be necessary.

Features:
Floodlit Range
Sauna
Lockers
Storage

Designer:
Folco Nardi

Opened:
1990

Photo: José Hidalgo
Courtesy Costa del Sol Tourist Board www.visitcostadelsol.com

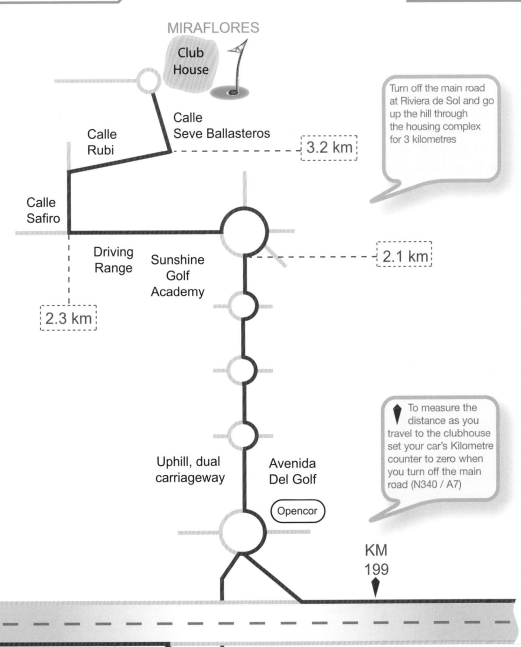

MIRAFLORES

Club House

Calle Seve Ballasteros

Turn off the main road at Riviera de Sol and go up the hill through the housing complex for 3 kilometres

3.2 km

Calle Rubi

Calle Safiro

2.1 km

Driving Range

Sunshine Golf Academy

2.3 km

Uphill, dual carriageway

Avenida Del Golf

To measure the distance as you travel to the clubhouse set your car's Kilometre counter to zero when you turn off the main road (N340 / A7)

Opencor

KM 199

Marbella Algeciras

KM 198

Cambio de Sentido

Fuengirola Malaga

RIVIERA DEL SOL

Map design © Kestrel 2005

9 holes

La Noria Golf Club

Tel: 952 587 653   Fax: 952 494 407

LLano de la Cala s/n
29649, La Cala de Mijas, Malaga

Features:
Driving Range
Lockers
Dressing Room
Lessons

Designer:
Francisco Navarro

Opened:
2003

This course offers enjoyable golf set amongst magnificent lakes and a stream. A further 9 holes are being developed.

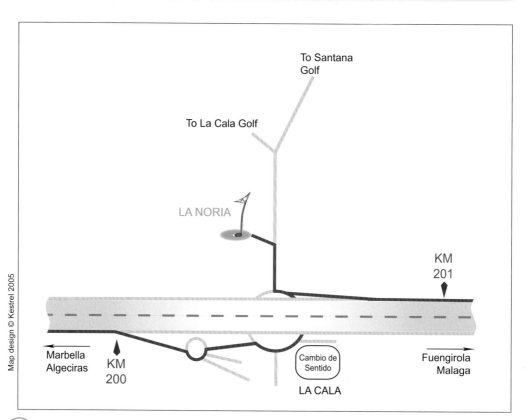

To Santana Golf

To La Cala Golf

LA NORIA

KM 201

Marbella
Algeciras

KM 200

Cambio de
Sentido

LA CALA

Fuengirola
Malaga

Map design © Kestrel 2005

HOTEL TAMISA GOLF

in the heart of the "Valley of Golf"

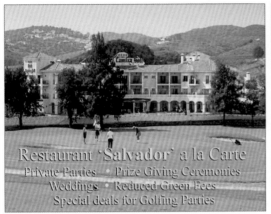

Hotel Tamisa Golf is small but comfortable, with 24 rooms and magnificent views of the golf course, spacious lounges and a conference room. We also have a Beauty Salon and wellness area with an indoor pool, Jacuzzi, sauna & gymnasium all open to the public.

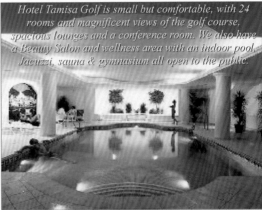

Restaurant 'Salvador' a la Carte
Private Parties • Prize Giving Ceremonies
Weddings • Reduced Green Fees
Special deals for Golfing Parties

Hotel Tamisa Golf - Camino Viejo de Coin km 3.3 - 29649
Mijas Costa (Malaga)
Tel: +34 952 585 988 - Fax: +34 952 663 893
Email: reservas@hoteltamisagolf.com
Web: www.hoteltamisagolf.com   www.weddingsintamisa.com

Hotel Tamisa Golf

La Cala Resort

La Cala Resort

Tel: 952 669 033   Fax: 952 669 034

La Cala de Mijas, Apdo. de Correos 106
29649 Mijas Costa, Malaga

golf@lacala.com
www.lacala.com

Features:
Hotel
Driving Range
Golf Academy
Squash / Tennis
Gym / Sauna
Lockers / Storage

Designer:
Cabell B.
    Robinson

Opened:
South 1991
North 1992

SOUTH

METRES	PAR	CV	SLOPE
5925	72	75.1	135
5412	72	68.8	128
4785	72	70.6	120
4467	72	69.1	117

NORTH

METRES	PAR	CV	SLOPE
6187	73	72.7	138
5782	73	70.5	132
5144	73	72.5	121
4759	73	69.3	119

A third 18-hole course is to be added to the North and South courses on La Cala Resort making a total of 54 holes – the largest golf complex on the Costa del Sol. This resort is also the home of the David Leadbetter Golf Academy which includes a six hole par-3 course.

Courtesy Costa del Sol Tourist Board www.visitcostadelsol.com

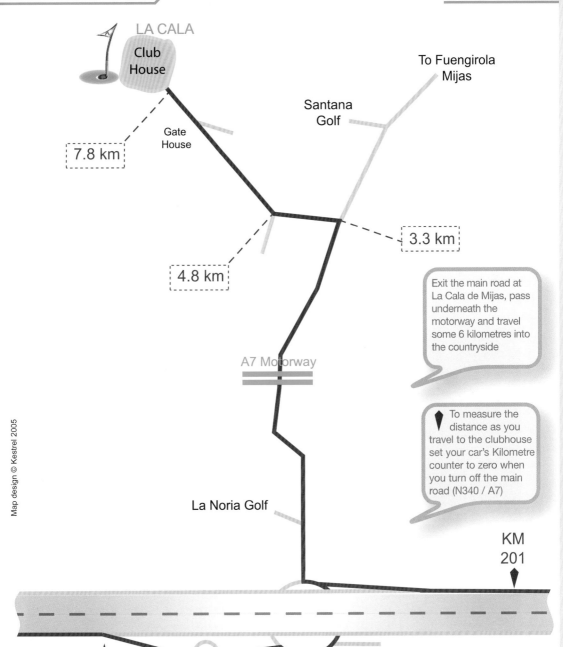

LA CALA

Club House

To Fuengirola Mijas

Santana Golf

Gate House

7.8 km

3.3 km

4.8 km

Exit the main road at La Cala de Mijas, pass underneath the motorway and travel some 6 kilometres into the countryside

A7 Motorway

To measure the distance as you travel to the clubhouse set your car's Kilometre counter to zero when you turn off the main road (N340 / A7)

La Noria Golf

KM 201

KM 200

Marbella Algeciras

Cambio de Sentido

Fuengirola Malaga

LA CALA

Map design © Kestrel 2005

Santana Golf & Country Club

Tel: 902 517 700   Fax: 902 518 800

Ctra. La Cala-Entrerrios s/n
Valle del Golf de Mijas

info@santanagolf.com
www.santanagolf.com

METRES	PAR	CV	SLOPE
5986	72		
5654	72		
5258	72		
4860	72		

The recently opened Santana Golf & Country Club has already established itself as one of the leading courses in the area with other facilities being added monthly. Now forming part of the ever-expanding Mijas Golf Valley.

Features:
New Temporary
Clubhouse

Designer:
Cabell B.
   Robinson

Opened:
2004

Photo: José Hidalgo

Courtesy Costa del Sol Tourist Board www.visitcostadelsol.com

SANTANA

Club House

To Fuengirola
Mijas

3.8 km

To La Cala Golf

3.3 km

Exit the main road at La Cala de Mijas, go underneath the motorway and travel some 5 kilometres into the countryside

A7 Motorway

To measure the distance as you travel to the clubhouse set your car's Kilometre counter to zero when you turn off the main road (N340 / A7)

La Noria Golf

KM 201

Marbella
Algeciras

KM 200

Cambio de Sentido

Fuengirola
Malaga

LA CALA

Mijas

Mijas Golf

Tel: 952 476 843   Fax: 952 467 943

Avda. Camino Viejo de Coin, km 3.5
29649 Mijas Costa, Malaga

info@mijasgolf.org
www.mijasgolf.org

Features:
Driving Range
Lockers
Storage
Theme Bar

Designer:
Robert Trent
   Jones Snr

Opened:
Los Lagos 1976
Los Olivos 1984

LOS LAGOS

METRES	PAR	CV	SLOPE
6367	71	71.6	110
6007	71	71.0	111
5148	71	70.6	110

LOS OLIVOS

METRES	PAR	CV	SLOPE
5840	70	71.0	115
5601	70	69.3	113
4877	70	69.5	114

Mijas Golf has 2 18-hole courses: Los Lagos (The Lakes) - has wide user-friendly fairways and very little rough but several water hazards. Buggies not essential. Los Olivos (The Olive Trees) - is a shorter, tighter and more demanding course with larger greens all to USGA specifications.

Courtesy Junta de Andalucia

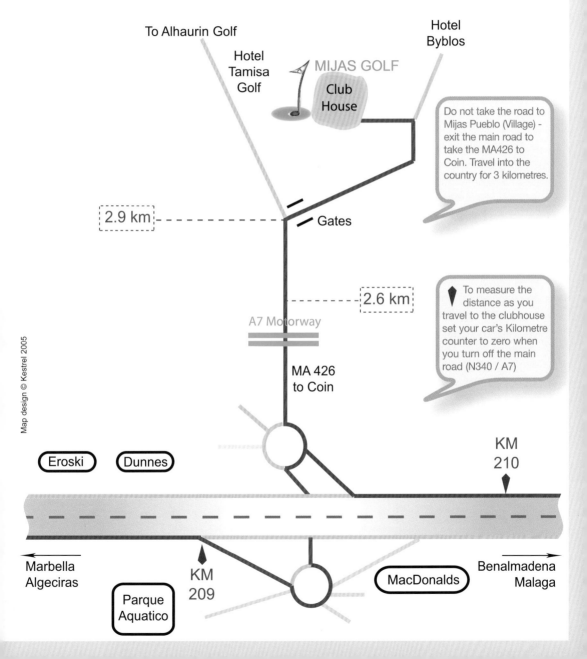

GOLF COURSES	MAP
Alhaurin	41
Torrequebrada	42
Parador Malaga	43
Lauro 27	44
Guadalhorce	45
El Candado	46
Añoreta	47

Miguel Toro

Lauro 27 Golf Club

AREA 6 The Area lies between Fuengirola to the west and the city of Malaga, and its airport, to the east. Alhaurin Golf lies inland, with Guadalhorce and Lauro 27 a little way from the main road, but Torrequebrada and Parador lie off the road near the airport. Añoreta is a few kilometres to the east of the city of Malaga. Most of the courses are set in rural surroundings, but urbanisations are being built-up. Main population centre is Malaga, capital of the province of Malaga, and inland are the country towns of Alhaurin la Torre and Alhaurin el Grande. Many of the inland villages in the area retain the style and charm of what are called Andalusian "white villages" with restaurants and cafes offering local dishes. The resort towns of Benalmadena and Torremolinos offer a wide selection of bars, cafes, restaurants, shopping and night-life.

...We'll get you
to the tee
on time !

CRGGOLF

PROBABLY
THE BEST GOLFING
HOLIDAY SET-UP ON THE COSTA DEL SOL
SPECIAL OFFERS
FIXED UNTIL 31ST DECEMBER 2006!!!!

7 NIGHTS ACCOMMODATION
6 DAYS BREAKFAST
TRANSFERS TO AND FROM MALAGA AIRPORT
TRANSFERS TO AND FROM THE GOLF COURSES
FREE USE OF LEADERBOARD FACILITY
CHALLENGE MATCH AGAINST THE LOCALS
(If you feel you are good enough!!!)
DISCOUNTED PRESENTATION DINNER AVAILABLE

3 ROUND PACKAGE
@£255 PER PERSON

**Golfing
Holidays in
the Sun**

4 ROUND PACKAGE
@£295 PER PERSON

**Free
Travel
Insurance**

5 ROUND PACKAGE
@£330 PER PERSON

AN EXTRA 10% DISCOUNT ON ALL WEEKLY PACKAGES TAKEN BETWEEN 15TH
NOVEMBER - 15TH DECEMBER & 2ND JANUARY - 31ST JANUARY

CRGGOLF MINI-BREAKS ALSO AVAILABLE
2 or 3 nights accommodation, breakfast, airport & golf course transfers
1 Round Package@ £175 or 2 Round Package@ £215

Courses to choose from On our Weekly & Mini-Break Golf Packages - Alhaurin, Anoreta,
Baviera, Guadalhorce, Lauro, La Noria, Miraflores or Parador - Other courses available with
small supplements
Please contact our Director of Golf in Spain Kevin Jenkins on (0034) 677806058
or e-mail crggolfspain@msn.com for Quotation or further information

CRGGOLF LTD. Registered in England at High Street Windsor Berkshire England (UK) SL4 1LD
*Free travel insurance available to all those without pre-existing medical conditions and under 65 years of
age - for those over 65 or with pre-existing medical conditions the relevant supplements will apply.

Alhaurin

Alhaurin Golf and Hotel Resort

Tel: 952 595 800   Fax: 952 594 586

Ctra. MA-426 Fuengirola/Coin Km. 15.1
29120 Alhaurin el Grande, Malaga

reservasgolf@alhauringolf.com
www.alhauringolf.com

METRES	PAR	CV	SLOPE
6220	72	72.0	130
5857	72	69.7	122
4941	72	70.2	118

A complete holiday centre, away from the Coast. Seve designed this amazing course in and around the mountains creating a paradise of breathtaking beauty just 15 km. inland from Fuengirola. The Junior Course may only be played by adults accompanied by a child!

Features:
Hotel, Sauna, Pool
Driving Range
9-Hole Par-3
18-Hole Junior
Nursery, Tennis
Equestrian Centre

Designer:
Seve Ballesteros

Opened:
1993

Photo: José Hidalgo

Courtesy Costa del Sol Tourist Board www.visitcostadelsol.com

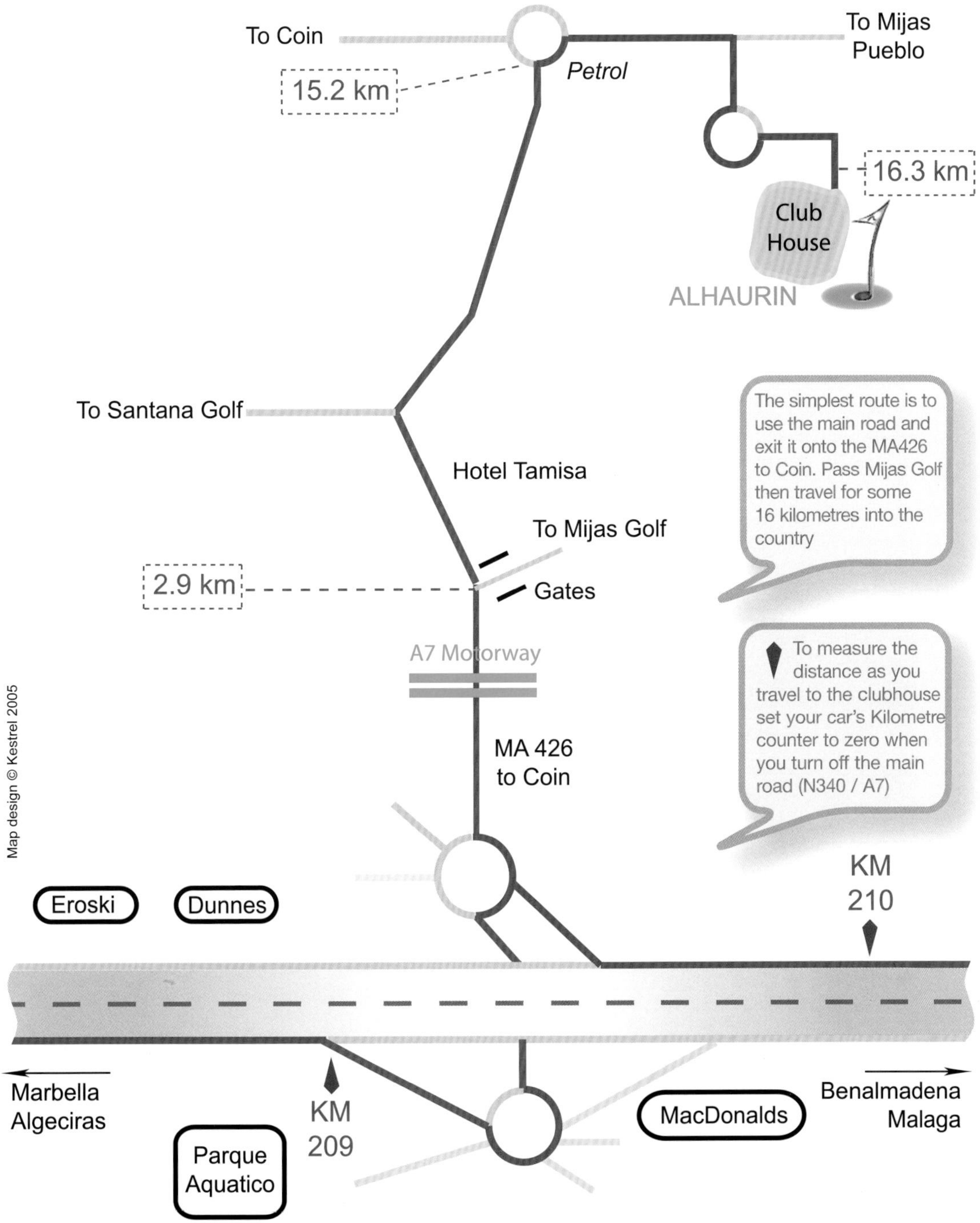

The simplest route is to use the main road and exit it onto the MA426 to Coin. Pass Mijas Golf then travel for some 16 kilometres into the country

To measure the distance as you travel to the clubhouse set your car's Kilometre counter to zero when you turn off the main road (N340 / A7)

Torrequebrada Golf

Tel: 952 442 742   Fax: 952 561 129

Urb. Torrequebrada, Edif. Club de Golf,
29630 Benalmadena, Malaga

bookings@golftorrequebrada.com
www.golftorrequebrada.com

METRES	PAR	CV	SLOPE
5852	72	70.7	134
5763	72	70.5	133
5021	72	71.3	124
4881	72	70.3	122

Host to several top tournaments, including the Spanish Open in 1979, this ever-popular course has been beautifully designed and features several outstanding holes. Stunning sea views make Torrequebrada very popular with visiting golfers.

Features:
Hotel
Driving Range
Pool, Tennis
Sauna,
Lockers / Storage

Designer:
Jose (Pepe)
  Gancedo

Opened:
1976

Photo: Miguel Ton...   ...urist Board www.visitcostadelsol.com

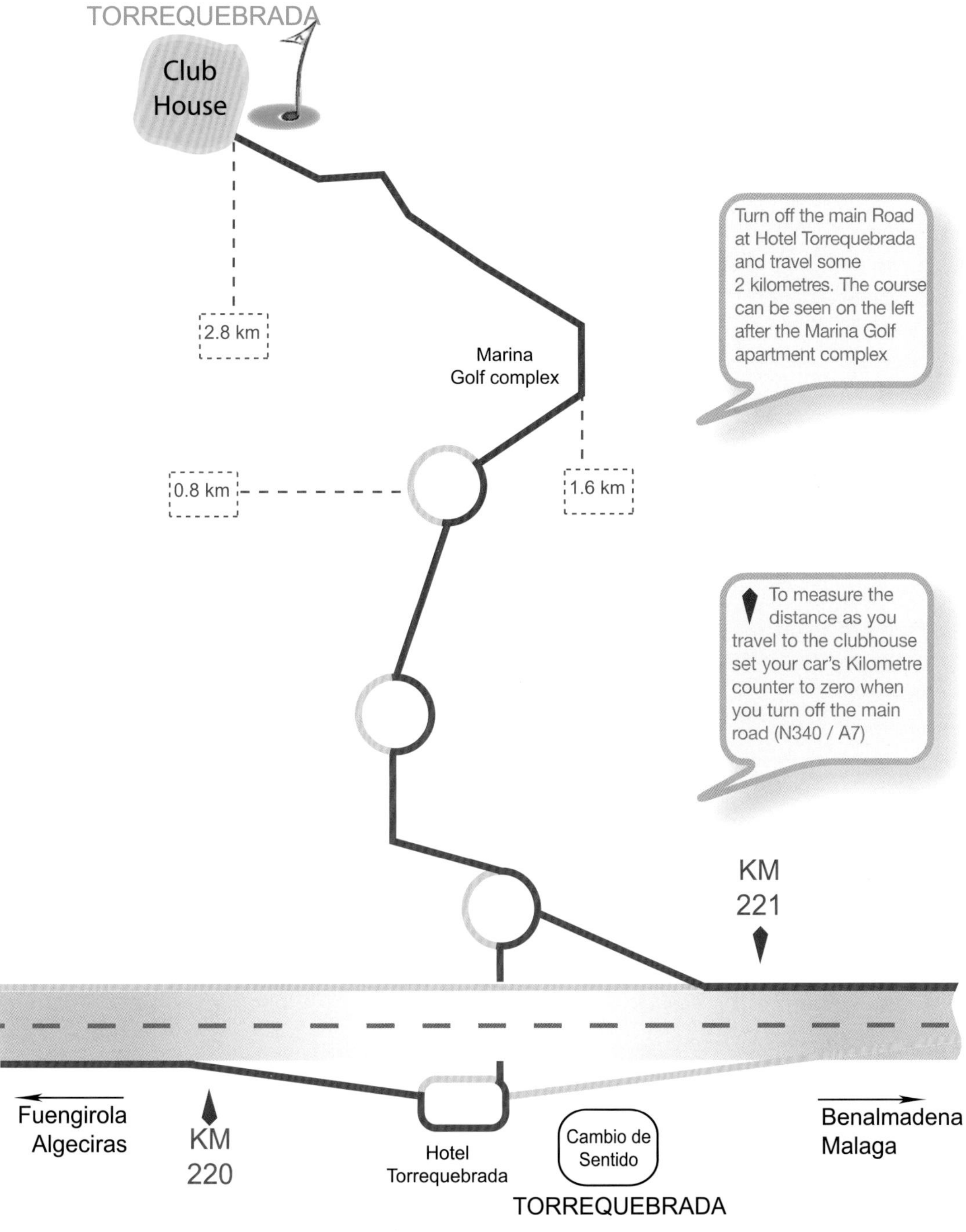

TORREQUEBRADA

Club
House

2.8 km

Marina
Golf complex

0.8 km

1.6 km

Turn off the main Road
at Hotel Torrequebrada
and travel some
2 kilometres. The course
can be seen on the left
after the Marina Golf
apartment complex

To measure the
distance as you
travel to the clubhouse
set your car's Kilometre
counter to zero when
you turn off the main
road (N340 / A7)

KM
221

Map design © Kestrel 2005

Fuengirola
Algeciras

KM
220

Hotel
Torrequebrada

Cambio de
Sentido

TORREQUEBRADA

Benalmadena
Malaga

Parador (Royal Malaga Golf Club)
Tel: 951 011 120   Fax: 952 372 072
Autovia Malaga-Algeciras, Malaga

malaga.golf@parador.es
www.parador.es

HOLES 1 - 18

METRES	PAR	CV	SLOPE
6173	72	72.3	127
6045	72	71.2	125
5361	72	72.9	122
5139	72	71.4	120

Features:
Hotel
Driving Range
Pool
Tennis

Designer:
Tom Simpson

Opened:
1925

HOLES 10 - 27

METRES	PAR	CV	SLOPE
5520	71		
5355	71		
4728	71		

It is reputed that Scotsman Tom Simpson designed Parador Golf for the King of Spain to play whenever he visited Malaga. It was the front-runner of all golf-courses built in Andalucia and has maintained a high standard over 80 years. The Paradores Group is state-owned.

HOLES 19 - 9

METRES	PAR	CV	SLOPE
5195	69		
5045	69		
4523	69		

Photo: Miguel Toro

Courtesy Costa del Sol Tourist Board www.visitcostadelsol.com

To Lauro Golf

AIRPORT

KM
230

Cadiz

To Bypass

Torremelinos
Algeciras

Malaga

MacDonalds

KM
229

To
Malaga
Cadiz

Railway

To measure the
distance as you
travel to the clubhouse
set your car's Kilometre
counter to zero when
you turn off the main
road (N340 / A7)

Motorway

0.8 km

Exit the main road near
Malaga Airport and go
under the main road
towards the sea for just
over 1 kilometre

1.3 km

Club
House

PARADOR

Mediterranean Sea

Map design © Kestrel 2005

Lauro 27 Golf

Lauro 27 Golf

Tel: 952 412 767   Fax: 952 414 757

Cortijo del Paredon, Los Caracolillos
A-366 Km.77, Alhaurin de la Torre, Malaga

info@laurogolf.com
www.laurogolf.com

Features:
Driving Range
Lockers
Caddies

Designers:
Folco Nardi &
Mariano Benitez

Opened:
1992

Lauro Golf has recently added another nine holes to its complex. The 27 holes are built in parkland just 12 km. inland from Malaga Airport and are user-friendly. It has a beautiful 200-year old farmhouse converted to a Clubhouse.

HOLES 1 - 18

METRES	PAR	CV	SLOPE
6070	72	72.0	135
5689	72	69.8	132
4864	72	70.7	126

HOLES 10 - 27

METRES	PAR	CV	SLOPE
6067	72	71.7	131
5645	72	69.4	131
4935	72	70.8	126

HOLES 19 - 9

METRES	PAR	CV	SLOPE
6003	72	71.8	135
5640	72	69.6	132
4891	72	71.0	125

Photo: Miguel Toro

Courtesy Costa del Sol Tourist Board www.visitcostadelsol.com

Area 6

MAP **44**

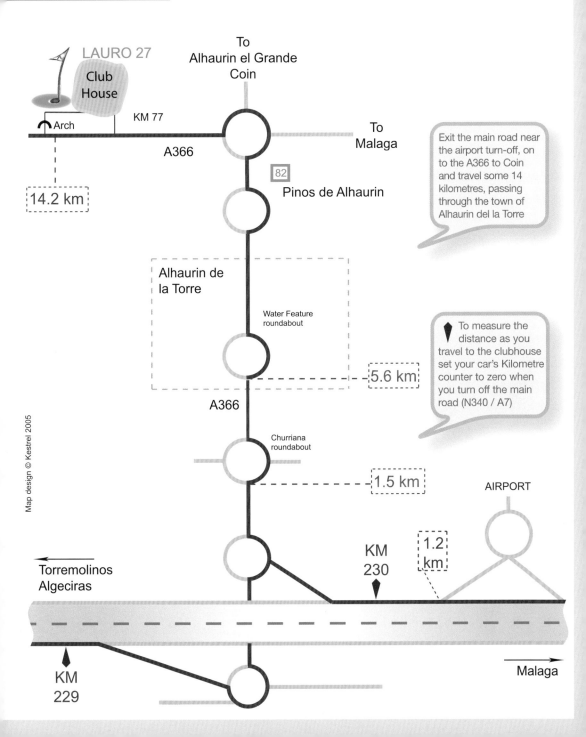

Guadalhorce

Guadalhorce Golf Club
Tel: 952 179 378   Fax: 952 179 372
Ctra. de Cartama, Km. 7
29590 Campanillas, Malaga
guadalhorce@golf-andalucia.net
www.guadalhorce.com

METRES	PAR	CV	SLOPE
6194	72	71.5	116
5860	72	69.6	116
5318	72	72.4	115
4992	72	70.3	112

Just 10km from Malaga Airport the delightful Guadalhorce Golf is a course of two halves – the outward nine holes is pleasant parkland with a more difficult back nine of raised greens and undulating fairways. The magnificent clubhouse is 18th century and is very impressive.

Features:
Driving Range
Pool
Tennis
Sauna
Nursery
Lockers / Storage

Designer:
Kosti Kuronen

Opened:
1988

Photo: Guadalhorce Golf Club

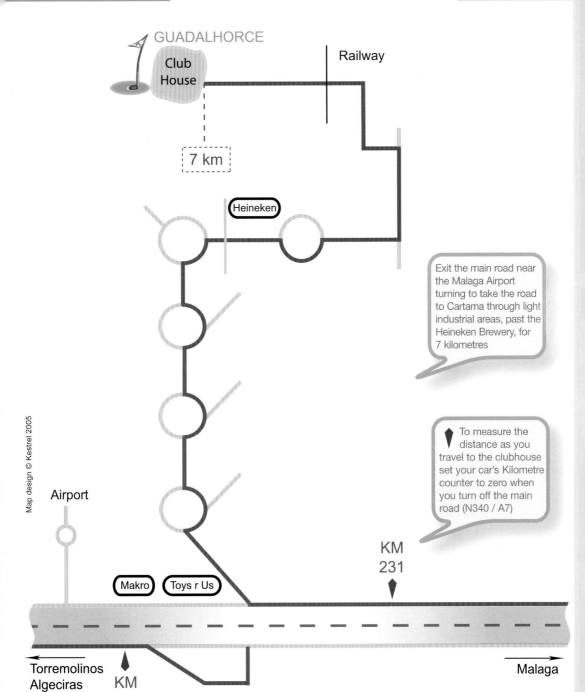

El Candado Golf

Tel: 952 299 340 Fax: 952 294 812

Urb. El Candado,
29018, Malaga

candado@golf-andalucia.net

Features:
Lessons
Club Rental

Designer:
Carlos Fdez. Caleya

Opened:
1968

Well-known to all levels of golfer, the course is situated in a small valley which gives it many differences of level and challenging greens.

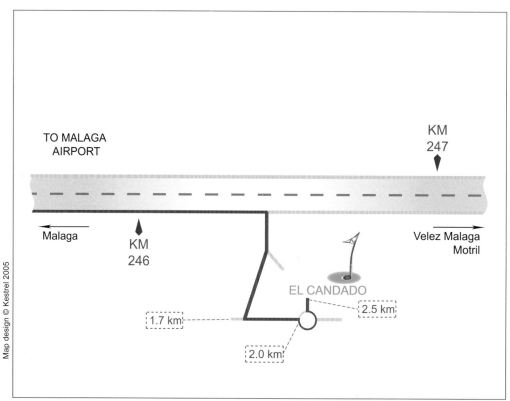

TO MALAGA
AIRPORT

KM
247

Malaga

KM
246

Velez Malaga
Motril

EL CANDADO

2.5 km

1.7 km

2.0 km

Map design © Kestrel 2005

Añoreta

Añoreta Golf

Tel: 952 404 000   Fax: 952 404 050

Avda. del Golf s/n
29730 Rincon de la Victoria, Malaga

anoreta@golf-andalucia.net
www.anoretagolf.es

METRES	PAR	CV	SLOPE
5976	72	71.3	134
5673	72	69.0	124
5175	72	72.3	124
4901	72	70.1	121

The second course built east of Malaga and the first designed by Cañizares of Ryder Cup fame. Water plays a big part in course management so beware ! The clubhouse is a lovely old building converted from days of the gentry.

Features:
Driving Range
Lockers
Storage
Sauna

Designer:
Jose-Maria
  Cañizares

Opened:
1990

Courtesy Junta de Andalucia

Take the N340 east,
pass the turn-off to
Malaga city, continue on
in the direction of
Almeria. The course is
on the south side of the
main road

To measure the
distance as you
travel to the clubhouse
set your car's Kilometre
counter to zero when
you turn off the main
road (N340 / A7)

KM
258

TO MALAGA
AIRPORT

← Malaga

KM
257

Velez Malaga →
Motril

0.2 km

Club
House

AÑORETA

Map design © Kestrel 2005

Understanding real estate terms

A real estate agent, *una agencia inmobiliaria*, acts to help to buy or sell your property and some may act as advisors, *gestores*, of real estate services, *servicios inmobiliarios*. A property bought off-plan, *sobre-plano*, can often be purchased at a discount, *un descuento*, directly from the developer, *el promotor*, before it is built. The legal details and signing of the contract, *el contrato de compraventa*, are carried out by the lawyer, *el abogado*. Land for building is bought in plots, *parcelas*, and is subject to planning permission based on the land being zoned as rural, *rustico*, or urban, *urbano*. The local Town Hall, *el Ayuntamiento*, controls real estate activity such as permissions, *permisos*, through its Planning Department, *el Departamento Urbanistico*.

Photo courtesy: www.pool-concept.com

• Listed here are a selection of the Spanish words, with their English equivalents, which you may come across in your transactions when setting up a home on the Costa del Sol.

Abogado	Lawyer	Mudanza	Removal
Acuerdo	Agreement	Muebles	Furniture
Adosada	Terraced	Notario	Public notary
Aire Acondicionado	Air conditioned	Obra	Works
Alquiler	Rent	Parcela	Plot
Apartamento	Apartment	Permiso	Permission
Atico	Penthouse	Piscina	Pool
Ayuntamiento	Town Hall	Piso	Apartment
Calefacción	Heating	Planta baja	Ground floor
Casa	House	Primera linea	Front-line
Casa Piloto	Show House	Promotor	Developer
Chalet	Villa	Reparación	Repair
Cocina	Kitchen	Residencia	Residence
Comprar	Buy	Seguro	Insurance
Construcciones	Constructions	Se vende	For sale
Disponible	Available	Sobre plano	Off-plan
Dormitorio	Bedroom	Solar	Building site
Esritura	Deeds	Suelo	Floor
Escuela	School	Techo	Roof
Finca	Landed Property	Terraza	Terrace
Gestor	Administrator	Trasferencia	Transfer
Gimnasio	Gym	Ventana	Window
Impuesto	Tax, Duty	Vista	View
Inmobiliaria	Estate Agency	Vivero	Plant nursery
Inversión	Investment	Vivienda	Dwelling

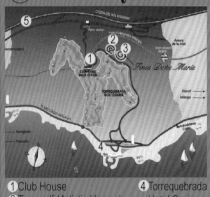

Time to take it easy . . . .

Many of the golfers playing on the Costa del Sol are residents having taken early retirement. For those visitors still preparing for that happy moment, the following helpful pointers may be of interest. Girlings Retirement Options Ltd specialise in retirement housing to rent throughout the UK, and now in Spain, on secure tenancies- here they present the following points which should be considered when exploring the course of action to take when planning for retirement -

Time to take it easy

Retirement offers time to play golf and pursue all those other activities you've been waiting to have time to enjoy - especially the time to relax.

"The healthiest development on the Costa del Sol - Sol Andalusi in Alhaurin El Grande"

Who can I talk to?

As we age we can find it gradually more difficult to cope with the day-to-day responsibilities of running a home. Gardening, window cleaning, general maintenance and housework can become some of the many increasing chores round the home. Add to this the loss of a partner, ill health and the day eventually arrives when you think - enough is enough.

But what to do?

Firstly you should consider your financial requirements and housing needs. Do you need such a large property? Would it more practical to down-size? What about moving into a purpose-built retirement apartment where the security and ease of running can give you a new lease of life? Or maybe you need a greater degree of assistance in a close-care or nursing scheme which provides more support in keeping with your increased frailty?

Renting as an option

Renting provides an opportunity to rent for as long as required with the full support of a professional organisation to assist you. Renting also provides the opportunity to try before you buy, and the flexibility to move easily should your circumstances change.

If you need to sell your present home and or would like to receive assistance to find a more suitable new one, together with advice on retirement options, you may find it useful to contact Girlings, at www.girlings.co.uk.

Advertisement Feature

Girlings
Retirement Options

Leaders in Retirement Rentals in the United Kingdom

are pleased to be able to offer studio, one and two bedroom apartments to rent at
Sol Andalusí Healthy Homes
at Alhaurín de la Torre near Málaga. All apartments are fitted out to a high standard and include comfort conditioning, marble floors, double-glazing, fitted kitchens with Bosch or AEG appliances and hydro massage showers or baths doubling as a jacuzzi. Facilities at Sol Andalusí include indoor and outdoor pools; restaurant, mini market, gymnasium, health spa, cinema, theatre and 24 hour medical care centre. A nine-hole golf course is proposed.

Rents *inclusive* of service charges range from €1,325 - €3,150 per month

Terms will vary according to length of lease up to 5 years by agreement

For further information visit www.girlings.co.uk
Telephone: +44 1823 346800 (In UK)
Email: girlings@telefonica.net

Or speak to Susana Moro at the Girlings Office in Sol Andalusí on
(+34) 952963127 (In Spain)
Email: susanamoro@telefonica.net

Visitors to the Costa del Sol are from many countries and the variety in places to eat reflects how international the Coast has become, but traditional Spanish cooking is available in many different types of establishment. Travellers on the Costa del Sol will always find open somewhere on the road to stop and eat throughout the day, except for the rest time from 4 pm to 7 pm. The *venta* or *meson* is a full restaurant with a bar serving *tapas*, the small portions of specialities from the *cocina*, the kitchen. Fish restaurants offer a varied choice of *pescado*, battered, *rebozado*, or fried, *frito*, and the meat restaurants offer *carne*, smoked *ahumado*, grilled, *asado* or *a la parilla*, and *a la plancha*, or perhaps try a dish such as *paella*. Enjoy with your meals the Spanish red wine, *tinto* or white, *blanco*, which will either be house wine, *de la casa*, or perhaps a wine of quality, a *reserva*.

Photo courtesy: Archivo Bonechi

Photos courtesy: www.visitacostadelsol.com

The sweet dark wines of Malaga are produced from sun-dried raisins and are enjoyed with a selection of different dishes . . .

...and is a favourite with a traditional dish like a sea-food *paella*

Useful Words

Listed here are a selection of the Spanish words, with their English equivalents, which you may come across whilst eating out or eating in, on the Costa del Sol.

Ahumado	Smoked	Niños	Children
Ajo	Garlic	Pan	Bread
Asador	Grill	Panaderia	Baker
Agua	Water	Parilla	Gridle
Agua con gas	Sparkling Water	Pastél	Cake
Agua sin gas	Still water	Pasteleria	Cake shop
Blanco	White	Patatas	Potatoes
Bollo	Bread roll	Patatas Fritas	Chips
Boquerón	Whitebait	Pavo	Turkey
Caramelos	Sweets	Pescado	Fish
Carne	Meat	Plancha	Hotplate
Cerveza	Beer	Platos rapidos	Fast dishes
Cebolla	Onion	Pollo	Chicken
Chorizo	Garlic sausage	Postre	Dessert
Chuletas	Chops	Pub	Night time bar
Cordero	Lamb	Queso	Cheese
Comida	Meal, food	Ración	Portion by plate
Comida para llevar	Take-away food	Rebozado	Battered
Desayuno	Breakfast	Refrescos	Refreshments
Ensalada	Salad	Salchichas	Sausages
Filete	Beefsteak	Solomillo	Sirloin steak
Frito	Fried	Sopa	Soup
Fritura	Fried fish	Supermercado	Supermarket
Grande	Large	Tapa	Small portion
Hamburguesa	Hamburger	Ternera	Veal
Hielo	Ice	Tienda	Shop
Helado	Ice-cream, frozen	Tinto	Red, wine
Huevos	Eggs	Tinto de verano	Red wine &
Jamon Serrano	Ham, cured		lemonade
Jamon York	Ham, sandwich	Tortilla	Omelette
Leche	Milk	Tortilla francesa	Omelette, plain
Legumbres	Vegetables	Venta	Country Inn
Mariscos	Shellfish	Verdura	Greens
Menú del Dia	Menu of the day	Vino	Wine
Menú economico	Special price menu	Vino reserva	Vintage wine
Mesón	Inn	Vino de mesa	Table wine

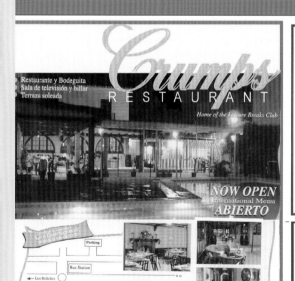